My Last Self-Help Book

A Journey from Anxiety and Depression to Emotional Health

Stephen McCourt

ISBN: 1-4528-4665-0
ISBN-13: 9781452846651

To Jane

Your guidance and support saved my life. When I was floundering in the waves of my emotion, you always pulled my head far enough above the water so that I could glimpse the shore.

"What is emotional health?"

When I asked this question of each of my many therapists, I never received a satisfactory answer. None could put a simple, workable definition into words and all but one of them thought that "emotional health" was a relative term, reflecting a concept that differed from person to person. In fact, all of them used the word "cope" instead of "enjoy."

Through my journey I learned the definition of emotional health. Simply put, a person is emotionally healthy when his or her emotions are vehicles for participating in life, rather than simply coping with it. A person who is emotionally healthy accepts that *all* emotions—love, hate, sadness, happiness, peace, worry, joy, anger and grief—are all parts of a healthy human psyche.

My Last Self Help Book

The Cost of Anxiety Disorders

Anxiety Disorders and Generalized Anxiety Disorder (GAD) are the most common mental illness in the United States, anxiety disorders affect more than 19 million adults who make up more than 13 percent of Americans in their prime—from 18 to 54 years of age.

The Anxiety Disorders Association of America (ADAA), commissioned a study called "The Economic Burden of Anxiety Disorders." This 2002 study, which was based on data gathered by the association and published in the *Journal of Clinical Psychiatry*, found that anxiety disorders cost the country more than $42 billion a year—almost one third of the $148 billion total mental health bill for the U.S. Further, the study asserts that nearly $23 billion of those costs are associated with the repeated use of healthcare services, as those with anxiety disorders seek relief for symptoms that mimic physical illnesses. For example, people with anxiety disorders are three-to-five times more likely to go to the doctor and six times more likely to be hospitalized for psychiatric disorders than non-sufferers.[1]

It Began

"The Irish are the only people completely impervious to psychoanalysis."
—Sigmund Freud

Ten years old, I was sitting on the beach on my family's green square of blanket and towels under the sun of a nice summer day when my sister went missing. Mom and Dad leapt up. With long, grown-up strides, they began to move across the sand in opposite directions, frantically searching for her while I remained seated, unmoving.

It's not that I didn't care about my sister. I was frozen. Sure that she was dead, I pictured an undertow snatching her out to sea. I saw her struggling against the seaweed as it dragged her under the waves. "Oh, my God," I cried, clapping my hands to my head. "Oh, my God!"

It was my first panic attack.

Today, as I recall that moment, I recognize the comic irony that my sister was perfectly fine, just wandering up the beach, while I never quite broke free of that moment. Panic and anxiety have dogged me ever since I was that 10-year-old boy, painfully anxious about losing my sister. Even when I felt relatively happy, the stress seethed just below the surface, casting its shadow over everything.

By the age of 45, I'd had a very successful life. I'd written two books, made a lot of money, had two wonderful daughters, traveled the world and started a company. I was a loving father, a loyal husband, a consultant to top corporations and an expert on human interactions. When I looked back on my life, I felt tremendous satisfaction on one level. But, on another, I saw it for what it was: a daily struggle to hold on.

An achiever, I was good at whatever I set my mind to. Throughout my business career and personal life, I proved that, through sheer force of will, I could achieve almost any goal. Applying my intellect and perseverance, I accrued substantial success such that my credentials impressed both clients and friends.

In spite of my accomplishments, I was afflicted with anxiety, depression and neurosis. My mind would not turn off and I couldn't remember a time when I wasn't worrying, obsessing or feeling depressed about something. So, while I could master anything I set my mind to, I could not master my own state of mind.

As I grew older, I noticed repeating patterns in my jobs, my relationships and in the rest of my life but, still, I felt powerless to stop them. Like most of my jobs, my marriages were interesting, at first, but eventually they became unfulfilling and routine. Depression struck twice—both times a couple of years into a new marriage. And, of course, there was the anxiety. Always, the anxiety.

I couldn't sit still, couldn't be alone with my thoughts. To escape, I kept myself very busy with projects, work, kids and relationships.

As I fought against my neurosis, I learned that my family history included depression and anxiety. All of my siblings, in fact, struggled with anxiety and depression and found themselves alone or in difficult relationships, unhappy with their partners.

I am sure that we appeared no different from other families that include some satisfactory marriages, some unsatisfactory ones, and some divorces. But the common thread in our family was unhappiness; no one in my family was "happy." The highest I would rate any of my family members was "relatively happy"—relative, say, to the misery that I felt much of the time.

I endured so much persistent anxiety and depression that, when I was a teenager, my mother paid for me to learn transcendental meditation to help me relax. (My anxiety must have been pretty bad for my mother, a devout Catholic, to pay for her son to practice Hinduism.)

Starting with my teenage years, I also drank regularly. Though I did not drink enough that I would classify myself as an alcoholic, alcohol helped me handle my anxiety and I did use it to self-medicate. And, of course, I also smoked pot and chased girls. Perfectly normal, perfectly healthy…Right?

My anxiety also manifested itself in physical signs. I had bad acne. I scratched and picked at myself constantly. Later in life, I developed psoriasis and several endearing nervous tics. I was not alone. All the McCourt's pick at ourselves. We all suffer from psoriasis. We all have nervous tics and twitches. And we all fight anxiety and depression. However, we each cope with our signs and symptoms differently. Some rely on prescribed medications, some on un-prescribed medications, if you know what I mean.

We believe that our family genes are the underlying cause of our distress. The DNA excuse—the "McCourt curse"—made sense. In some ways, it is comforting to blame our problems on our genetics and, even today, most of my siblings believe it is the price we pay for being in our family.

I would still believe it, too, if my symptoms hadn't disappeared. But the truth is that, today, I am a fundamentally different person with a fundamentally different life. My life is peaceful. My psoriasis and nervous twitches are gone. I no longer crave alcohol and drink only sparingly. And, while I still worry, my anxiety level is very low, with concern that is appropriate to the specific situation. Noticing how much I have changed, my friends, children and loved ones can see the difference in my life.

A couple of years ago, the shadow of my depression lifted, and I don't think it will return. Today, in the last stages of a very difficult emotional process, I am almost finished with the emotional work needed to heal very old wounds. The journey to this place was difficult, painful, exhausting and dangerous—and well worth it. The behaviors that I once thought were intractable parts of my biochemical makeup have slowly slipped away, leaving me relaxed and peaceful. I no longer fret and obsess about things over which I have little or no control. Instead, I now experience happiness that is unlike anything I ever expected.

In the past, I kept moving so that I wouldn't have to confront my life and all its dysfunctions. Now, I don't have to do that anymore. It's not that my motivation has gone away, but that I no longer have to prove anything or escape anything.

"Slaying the dragon," "facing your demons," "self-actualization," the "hero's journey..." Before I set out to accomplish the work of the past few years, I used these terms myself. I didn't have a clue how much these trite, shallow and insulting aphorisms trivialized the struggle—not that they aren't true. They are. They're just so simplistic when they spill out of the mouths of people who haven't covered the ground and done the work. In other words, *"What doesn't kill you makes you stronger"* is something only survivors have earned the right to say.

This journey—this metamorphosis—is like shedding your skin in order to grow. Looking back on it, I recognize that I might never have started on this path if I'd really known how difficult it would be. So I respect people's fear of this journey.

But what lies on the other side is a different existence—and it *is* worth it.

4

Trust

To complete this journey, *you have to trust.*

You do not have to trust your mother, your spouse, your therapist or your god, but you *do* have to trust your psyche, the process and yourself. Without placing your trust in your journey, you cannot reach the other side; the process will be impossible to complete.

Imagine that you are swimming toward a destination that is masked with fog. Though you cannot see your destination, you must trust that it is there as you swim away from the security of the shore behind you. Family, friends, therapists and lovers tried to convince me that there *was* no other side, that I was swimming into a vast ocean that was too rough and dangerous to cross—like Columbus sailing towards the edge of the Earth. They were right about that ocean; it *is* dangerous. But there *is* some solid ground out there in that fog—another beach waiting to receive you—and the only way to find it is to swim so hard on your way across that you save nothing for the swim back.

Having completed that swim, I now humbly ask for your trust, for no matter what you have heard from your family, friends or therapist:

It *is* possible to be happy—not *relatively* happy, but *happy happy.*

Today, I am again on dry land and I can tell you that it *is* possible to have fulfilling intimate relationships and to feel a deep sense of connection with people and the world. It *is* possible to live free from anxiety and depression. It *is* possible to live a fulfilling, passionate life.

As you begin this process, you probably have an idea about what will make you happy. You may be hoping for a loving relationship, a child, a new job, financial security or better health, so your motivation in this process may be to find the happiness you've longed for all your life. But, while you think you know what will make you happy, the fact is that you don't *really* know what you want.

You probably find this difficult to believe and, worse, arrogant. But, until you dive into that water and swim into that fog—and until you reach the solid earth on the other side—the elements that you believe will make you happy mean nothing. I suggest that, while you are flailing out there in the water, you suspend your belief in the pot of gold. Your desires will only get in the way of the process.

But don't despair because, if you do finish the journey, you *will* achieve happiness. Just keep in mind these basic principles of trusting your psyche, the process and yourself:

You will not get the things you want; you will replace them with things that you did not even know you wanted.

You will not answer your questions; you will answer questions you had not even thought of.

And the happiness at the end of your journey will not be the joy you expected.

Trust me. I swam away from shore into the thickest fog and made it to the other side and I know that the journey is worth it.

Rocket

"Can any human being ever reach that kind of light?"

— Indigo Girls

My friend Rocket ran so fast that, in soccer, he could chase down any player on the opposing team and steal the ball; thus the name Rocket. The most well adjusted person I have ever known, Rocket never seemed to struggle to adjust to anyone or anything. As far as I could tell, Rocket is completely free of neuroses, anxiety or depression and, to him, life looked effortless. He met his soul mate Ella, in college and 25 years later, their relationship remains my only model of happy, mature companionship.

But after college Rocket and I grew apart. I tried to keep contact but he didn't return my calls and let the friendship go. Frustrated and angry, I eventually gave up.

Rocket rejected me. I don't believe that he rejected me on purpose or even consciously—he would never do that—but now (and, only now) I finally understand that I made him feel uncomfortable with my anxious, codependent and neurotic worldview. I peppered him with questions that probably made no sense to him.

"What does it take to be happy?" I would ask. "Do you ever worry about people liking or disliking you?" and "Do you ever wonder about the meaning of life?" At times, I would quiz him about his relationship. "How did you know Ella was the one?" I asked. "How can anyone stay with the same person for an entire lifetime? Do you ever think about cheating on her?"

Rocket was my first indicator that emotionally healthy people don't mix well with those of us who are emotionally unhealthy. He taught me that people do not fall along an imaginary continuum from relative happiness to unhappiness. Rocket, for example, wasn't on a continuum. He wasn't even aware that there was such a thing. He was just happy. He was just living his life.

For that reason, Rocket—and people like him—have nothing to gain from this book. As different as Rocket's world was to me, the world of anxiety, neurosis and healing must also be foreign to him. As far as I know, he's never read or considered reading a self-help book. They just aren't on his radar. Rocket and others like him would not understand my process, my struggle, and my reasons for writing about my journey.

Still, his life gave me hope. If we were all like Rocket, I thought, maybe there wouldn't be so much unhappiness in the world. But I never thought I could reach the place where Rocket lives. It seemed too far, too inaccessible. While most of my life has been an expression of my neuroses, Rocket doesn't think about life. He just lives it. His life is an expression of who he is.

Many times, when I came close to giving up my journey, Rocket's life helped to keep me going. When I wanted to swallow a medication so that I could forget, or when my friends, family and therapists discouraged me, I always came back to Rocket and his life, which helped me believe in a better existence, in the far shore. That's where Rocket lived—a place where life flowed and relationships were natural and fulfilling. I saw that I could get there. I just had to keep on swimming.

After a very long and difficult swim, I have reached that shore. The search that drove me for so many years is ended and the demons of my neurosis no longer haunt me. I no longer have to keep moving to avoid falling down.

This is my *last* self-help book.

Truth

*"The opposite of a shallow truth is a falsity.
The opposite of a profound truth is another profound truth."*

—Albert Einstein

As I did my emotional work, a number of truths revealed themselves to me. They are not new. Other people discovered them before I did but, in all my research, I never found a collection of these truths together in one place. For this reason, I organized this book around those truths.

To those who have reached the other shore, these truths will seem self-evident. But, to those who have yet to complete their work, these truths will have a different effect. They will make some people angry. Some will grow defensive or frightened. I believe that these negative reactions occur because people have an inkling of the price they must pay to be truly happy.

Facing the truth is difficult. I spent my life rejecting the truth—fighting it and running from it. Facing the truth is uncomfortable. Truth mirrors our dysfunctions, unhappiness and self-deception and, when we look at it, we see the flaws and sadness that hold us. It takes courage, hope, perseverance and faith to look deeply into the pain we cause others and ourselves, but this vision is required if we are to know the truth.

I wrote this book for people who are brave enough to face the truth in their lives, people who have the courage to honestly face their own dysfunctions and, then, to commit to becoming happy.

I do not say this lightly. Many so-called experts, whose personal lives are a mess, freely advise other people about how to run their lives. Those "experts" are charlatans, hypocrites and snake-oil salesmen. Self-help gurus or coaches, weekend seminars, quick-fix schemes and medications do *not* offer truth. Rather, they are crutches that delay us from facing our truth.

On the other hand, facing the truth—and truth alone—is a Herculean task that provides a way out of misery, depression and anxiety as you come face-to-face with your life. Worth every tear, every sleepless night, every wrenching emotion, the quest for the truth is the most fulfilling process a human can experience.

Truth is not opinion, conjecture or point of view, and it is neither arrogant nor confrontational. Truth is truth. Truth belongs to all of us.

The First Truth

The only way to escape anxiety and depression is through deep and difficult emotional work. You can't *think* your way to emotional health.

The road to emotional health is long and hard, and it doesn't have a shortcut. Anyone who tries to steer you to an easier route is leading you astray and even therapists who promise quick relief are fooling you. The *only* path to a life of true happiness—free of anxiety and depression—is through deep and difficult emotional work.

The Second Truth

**You can't escape anxiety and depression on your own.
You need help.**

The work you must do to reach the other side is deep, difficult and exhausting. To get there, you need a guide, a person who has already traveled the path before you. While each individual's path to healing is unique, only someone who has traveled the path can guide you through your unique process.

The Third Truth

**In order to move past depression and anxiety,
you *must* break with the family in which you grew up.**

The patterns that make your life unhappy started when you were very young. In order to see them, change and heal them, you will need perspective. You can only reach an objective view of your unfulfilling patterns by breaking with the relationships that replicate your past.

The Fourth Truth

You are not in control of the healing process. The more you try to control the process, the longer it takes to reach the other side.

You will move forward in the process only by embracing your feelings. To do this, you must accept that the process will be emotional, ambiguous and scary. The more you try to suppress and control your emotions, the more they surface through anxiety, depression and compulsion.

The Fifth Truth

**As you do your work,
the true sources of your anxiety and depression will reveal themselves.**

The patterns in our lives that make our relationships, jobs, and personal lives either fulfilling or unfulfilling are emotional patterns set up when we were very young. We cannot identify and change these patterns through *intellectual* understanding; only *emotional* work will reveal, heal and significantly alter the direction of our lives.

The Sixth Truth

**If we don't do our work,
we pass on our anxious and depressive patterns to our children.**

Teenage mothers raise teenage mothers. Violent, abusive fathers create violent, abusive sons. Anxious parents have anxious children. The patterns repeat themselves through the generations until someone commits to shattering the mold. Only by doing our emotional work can we significantly change our children's future and help them to be truly happy.

The Seventh Truth

**The happiness you get when you reach the other side
is not the happiness you expected.**

Just like our unhealthy patterns are invisible to us, so too are the healthy patterns of intimacy and connectedness. Our neuroses keep us from seeing how happy we can be. Until we do our work, we are unaware of the amount of energy we use fighting for and against intimacy.

The Catch

There is only one way to determine if my words are true. You cannot be sure until you undertake the journey, until you work through the process. So, for those of you who decide to swim, the following pages contain an honest description of my own emotional journey. It is an intensely personal account of my struggle, pain and triumph. I hope it will inspire you to either swim for your life or be satisfied with the status quo.

I do not judge which path you choose…both are painful.

Swimming From Shore

"And even in our sleep, pain that cannot forget falls drop by drop upon the heart, until, in our own despair and against our will, comes wisdom to us through the awful grace of god."

—Aeschylus

On some deep level, uncharted by psychology or physiology, I realized that I was sick. I had a sickness. I kept my sickness at bay with noise—the noise of alcohol, of relationships, of my children and of my work. But, deep down, I was frightened. The silence was unnerving and I was afraid to see my life for what it was.

I filled the silence with alcohol. Not too much, just a beer before dinner, a glass of wine with my meal, and another beer before bed. I gave myself *just* enough of a buzz to fill the silence. I filled the silence with relationships, too, filling another's silence with mine and filling my silence with another. I filled the silence with work by keeping busy, always creating another project, checking off items on my to-do list, planning, prioritizing and always moving forward. I filled the silence with my children and family chores—laundry, dishes, home projects, driving here and there—and I filled it with TV and music. I filled my life with everything I could, *anything* that would allow me to avoid the silence, to avoid confronting myself. I created noise to avoid the painful work that I would need to do in order to heal. The louder the noise, the better I coped. Work harder…Drink harder…Parent harder…

The sickness grew louder and louder until, finally, silence drowned out all the noise. The silence broke me.

I ended up in a psych ward, a "behavioral health unit." Though I was a high-powered entrepreneur, author, lover, husband and father, I ended up playing cards with depressed retirees, manic-depressives and psychopaths.

The doctors said I was exhausted, and I was, but I was not exhausted from all that I was doing and all that I had accomplished. I was exhausted from trying to keep the silence at bay, from avoiding my sickness and pain. Maintaining the noise distanced me from my fears and protected me from my anger, grief, sadness and uncertainty, but it was too hard, even impossible, for me to keep it up.

The doctors tried drugs—anti-anxiety meds and anti-depressives—but these simply substituted one type of noise for another. The quiet loomed, waiting patiently for yet another distraction to subside. Indeed, when the drugs lost their potency, the silence returned, a yawning chasm that waited for me to accept and surrender. Finally, in despair and exhaustion, I let it overtake me.

It started with a break.

Somehow, I knew that I had to take this journey alone. I recognized that, to grow past anxiety and depression, I needed to break with my past and with my old patterns of who I was. But, since these patterns were invisible to me, I had to earn the perspective from which I might be able to see them. I recognized that I could earn that perspective and become whole only by doing very difficult work and by leaving some parts of myself behind. To heal and move forward, I needed to leave my past behind. To really do that, it was not enough for me to break with the patterns that defined me, but I had to break with my family, friends and lovers—with Mom and Dad, sisters, brothers, and lovers.

For all of us, the process of growing up, of individuation, *should* (but often doesn't) include the difficult step of separation. This separation, and all the pain that must go with it, is an important first step in the therapeutic process, as it was for me. I needed to cut myself off from the past. In my case, this meant I needed to set and maintain boundaries between myself and the people who raised me.

I had no one to rely on, no one to help. It was just me. Alone.

Cutting the vines and breaking free in this way triggered deep and painful feelings and intense emotions. What began as a trickle quickly grew into a torrent of uncontrollable grief, bone-deep sadness, vicious anger and maddening ambiguity.

Thus began the process of healing.

Crushing Grief

If I'd had the choice, I would have passed on the grief.

It came in waves, catching me off guard and shoving into my consciousness raw images of childhood, adolescent and adult wounds. My grief—of unhealthy attachments and savage detachments—was more terrifying and painful than I ever imagined as I exposed layers upon layers of repressed emotion and suppressed humanity. All the hurts of a lifetime forcibly injected into my psyche's frontal lobes, exploding into unstoppable tears, wrenching sobs, muscle-pulling spasms. Uncontrollable paroxysms of deep anguish slowly spent themselves, leaving me exhausted and bone weary.

I was more present than I'd ever been…unfortunately.

Vicious Anger

Then came anger.

Like a wildfire killing everything in its path, brutal anger and rage swelled within me, unrestrained by guilt, compassion or remorse. My violators became dartboards as I burned photographs, smashed mementos and purged memories. Symbolically, I was burning bridges, tearing down the old vines and melting the hooks that held me. Killing the past and, with it, all that I once held dear, I was scorching the earth to prepare for new growth.

Bone-Deep Sadness

Then sadness.

I cut myself off. Having lost everything—my friends, my family, my world, my mirrors, myself—I carried the sadness inside, everywhere: through the airport, to the movies, in my car. Like cheap sunglasses, the sadness blankets my life with an ugly yellow, off-color tint. I slowly accept that, eventually, I might not notice it as much, but my sadness—no longer repressed—would never go away. Now and forever, the world is different and sadness is again part of my life and part of me.

Maddening Ambiguity

And then I no longer have the answers. I don't know…I just don't know…

I *used* to know. I used to know a *lot*. I knew how to get things done. I knew how to be a good parent. I knew how corporations could be more successful. I always, always, always, always knew what to do next, the type of relationship I wanted, the type of work I was good at, the next line I would write.

I used to know so much.

But, then, I didn't know anymore. I didn't know what to do with my life. I didn't know what kind of father I would be to my children. I didn't know if I ever enjoyed my career. I didn't know what to look for in a healthy relationship.

It scared me. Not knowing is scary because I felt that I was *supposed* to know. It's what I *do* and who I *am*: I *know*. But, having broken the clinging vines of my family of origin, I was left with quiet—ambiguous and uncertain quiet, where nothing pushed or pulled and where nothing motivated me to begin again.

And then…

A Roaring Silence

The silence looked me in the eye and challenged me not to *know*, to just *be*. It challenged me to see myself as I really am.

Finally, painfully, reluctantly, I let go. And then, ever so slowly, the miracle presented itself. Standing in awe of the miracle that is my life, I see it. For some unfathomable, incredible, mystical reason I have life. The fever breaks and the sickness passes and I see that *I am*. It is a good place to start.

If this passage does not frighten you, you were not paying close enough attention.

The First Truth

The only way to escape anxiety and depression is through deep and difficult emotional work. You can't think your way to emotional health.

"How did I come to this? I dreamed myself a thousand times around the world but I can't get out of this place."

—Dave Matthews

I realized I'd gone too far in searching for answers when I found myself reading the book, _Mutual Causality in Buddhism and General Systems Theory_[2]. Though this is a good treatise on the link between Buddhist beliefs in seemingly unrelated, serendipitous occurrences and the same events in complex systems, it was a bit far a field for my purpose, which was to figure out the source of my panic attacks.

I've been searching for the answer to my anxieties and depression all my life, at times more obsessively than at others. My quest started with self-help books. When I was growing up in the 1970s, I read just about every self-help book available. At the time, bookstore shelves displayed a proliferation of books on self-esteem, from _I'm OK, You're Okay_ and _How To Be Your Own Best Friend_ to _The Road Less Traveled_ and _New Guide to Rational Living_, among many others.

I was obsessed. I even gave self-help books to friends and family so they could be happy, too. One Christmas, I gave my sister a copy of _How to Be Your Own Best Friend_ as a present. While my intentions were good, I didn't realize at the time that not only was it a neurotic thing to do, it also might have been a hurtful gift; getting a self-help book from your brother is like being told that you need this book because you're not okay.

I started to make a list of all the titles I've read, but I gave up after I reached 50 of them. Though all of those books helped me at least a little, I thought the list might make me look obsessive. Still, I continued searching for newer and better self-help titles and, as a result, read works by some of the great psychological thinkers: Sigmund Freud, Carl Jung, Aaron Beck, Albert Ellis and others who started the modern psychotherapy movement. Their writings provided me with many years' worth of reading material and gave me a good background in psychology and the therapeutic process. By reading their books and others, I came to understand different counseling techniques and theories, including cognitive and behavioral therapies, Rational Emotive Therapy (RET), psychodynamic psychotherapy, rebirthing and many, many others. So many theories, so little time. Since the writers were prolific, I always had another book to read and, consequently, I learned a lot about psychological disorders. And they scared the hell out of me.

When my sister attended nursing school, she learned about diseases and then would freak out whenever she got sick, because her symptoms always seemed to match the early onset of whatever disease she was studying at the time. I experienced the psychological version of this. Though I had never heard strange voices, when I read about schizophrenia, I feared that I might start hearing voices that told me to do weird things. Researching paranoia, I worried that I might begin to worry about people wanting to get me. The only symptom that I knew I didn't have was self-mutilation, unless it counts that I was biting my fingernails until they bled...

Though I started the self-help quest in search of answers, knowing so much turned out to be worse than not knowing. Reading the newspaper, whenever I learned about someone who had done something crazy, I wondered if I was capable of doing the same thing. Eventually, I was grateful when one of my books informed me that anxiety could make me anxious but it couldn't make me crazy. That reassured me and made me feel better.

During my self-help quest, I researched the therapeutic role of medications from lithium to Prozac and Buspar to XANAX. In the process, I entered a wonderland of psychopharmacological research as I tried several anti-anxiety drugs, mostly benzodiazepines. I also tried selective serotonin reuptake inhibitors (SSRIs) that suppress the brain's re-uptake of serotonin, which many say "causes" anxiety. Medications like Prozac, Paxil, Zoloft and many more enjoy a huge market and huge profits, though we have little knowledge of how they work. The doctors who prescribed them to me said that I could expect a bit of a "pop" (as they called it) when I first started. However, I was unpleasantly surprised to realize that the "pop" was jitteriness and anxiety. *Didn't I have enough anxiety?* I thought. *Now I'm taking a pill that induces anxiety?*

My research, of course, would not have been complete if I had neglected the therapy route. My first adult panic attack launched me on a fruitless search for the right counselor as I tried to deal with my symptoms by spending a great deal of time and money in one-on-one counseling. It was an interesting journey.

My very first counselor sat on a rug, burned incense and chanted. Though he was actually licensed to practice in the State of Washington, his approach was to identify and heal my chakras. *This is therapy?* I wondered. At the end of that first session, he told me that I was deeply disturbed and needed to see him every day for two weeks—at $75 a pop—or I might end up in a hospital. And he didn't even have a couch! I left, fully aware that we would never see each other again.

Next came the counselor who liked to talk about his boat. I learned quite a bit about sailing and boat maintenance and, since he audio taped each session so that I could listen to it between appointments, I also have an excellent tape library for reference. He also gave me a personality test and apparently decided that the best way to help me deal with my emotional pain and anxiety was to point out my personality deficiencies. The test results indicated my tendency towards histrionics and over-sensitivity to criticism. He might have considered these results before giving me the answers but, of course, he didn't and, per my diagnosis, I took it personally and my anxiety ratcheted up.

In desperation, I crossed the country seeking help. To augment my therapy, my therapists had referred me to the books of an internationally known psychologist and author whose writing led me to believe that he might have the answers. In his writings, he came across as a together guy with many of the answers I was seeking about the origins of anxiety and worry, how to cope with depression, and so on. His office was in New York City, so I scheduled a session with him while on a business trip to the East Coast. I was very excited and hopeful… until I met him. Without wearing shoes or socks, he sat curled up on a recliner and popped Maalox every few minutes. He made *me* nervous.

"You expect too much from life," he told me. "If you accept the fact that life is shit you'll feel better. Lowering your expectations is the key to happiness."

I began to suspect that the quality control standards in the mental health field needed work.

In spite of the setbacks, I did find some short-term relief and developed a good understanding of my prognosis: persistent depressive episodes accompanied by generalized anxiety disorder and panic attacks. This meant I tended to become depressed when stressed, but my anxiety was not tied to any specific pending situation. Rather, it was "general"! While I knew that my depressions came on when my marriages were ending (or should have been ending), I wondered how I could have just *general* anxiety, without a *cause*? How could anxiety simply *occur*? I thought, *"This is not good."*

Losing hope in the first bout of therapists, I resumed my everyday life. Sometimes, I felt good, even close to happy. I enjoyed being a caring father and a loving husband, and sometimes I found my work rewarding, up to a point. But the good times never lasted. Eventually, my anxious and depressed feelings returned or yet another problem with my relationships, job, or life interrupted my fleeting feelings of happiness. Back to the counselor I went.

I began to feel that I'd constantly be on the roller coaster, with temporary highs always being cut short by more desperation. I wondered if it was impossible to find a permanent answer to my problem.

Looking for a lasting fix, my next step was religion. Perhaps, I reasoned, it offered the answer. I read the Bible but found it too dogmatic. I tried Buddhism but it rejected emotion. I tried Hinduism but it rejected meat. I tried Taoism and missed the…Well, I'm sure I missed *something* but Taoism is so nondescript.

I also struggled with the "exclusionary clause" that many religions share: If you don't believe everything they say, then you are out! No soup for you! Each religion also asked me to give up the search, to rely only on faith, but I had to rely on *their* faith, not on any of the others. I couldn't do that. To rely solely on faith in god was to abandon my search, to give up my neurotic quest, which was the only thing that was keeping me sane, for god's sake!

Furthermore, to me, faith seemed like an easy way out. While I wanted the answers to life, faith just posed more questions and, thus, faith did not offer happiness.

Faith didn't offer happiness. Faith seemed like an easy way out. No answers to life—just more questions.

Of course, I couldn't neglect philosophy—it might have some answers! Joseph Campbell, Aquinas, Nietzsche, Fritjof Capra, the Dalai Lama, Camus, Huxley, Jack Kerouac, Adrienne Rich. (Obsess much?) Great bunch of guys and gals, but no answers.

But their existential angst made me feel right at home. One thing about philosophy—you may not be able to rely on it for answers, but it does offers plenty of questions. Every time a philosopher thinks up an answer, another thinker comes along and pokes holes in it. (I think therefore I am. So logically, a tree doesn't think so it isn't?)

Frustrated, then, I turned to science. Perhaps if I understood the physical world to a microscopic level then the answer would reveal itself to me. If I saw how the subatomic world worked perhaps, then, I could see the "hand of god" and that might make me happy. I jumped into quantum physics and systems theory. Talk about generating more questions!

For example, did you ever hear of the Heisenberg Uncertainty Principle? Werner Heisenberg discovered that you couldn't measure both the location and speed of an electron at the same time. By measuring an electron's location you changed its speed; by measuring its speed you changed its location. In other words, he found that you can't study something without changing it in some way. What if that applied to my search? If I changed my anxiety by trying to understand its origins, then my search was the ultimate dog-chasing-its-tail problem. Every time I thought I seized the answer between my teeth, it changed! That didn't give me much of a chance…

Next, I turned to the self-help gurus, starting with Tony Robbins. Mr. Infomercial, who has big, horsey teeth and who believes in Personal Power, is now being sued by his franchisees. I also turned to Stephen Covey, who wrote *The Seven Habits of Highly Effective People*. Covey self-righteously preaches that, to be a good person, you must spend more time with your children than with work; if you don't, then you are insufficient as a parent and as a person. *What about the people who work long and hard hours to make a better life for their children?* I reasoned. *Are they bad parents?* In the end, I found some good stuff but all of these self-proclaimed experts just seem so judgmental, self-righteous and smug. And, while they did not give me the answers, my anxiety continued to scream at me.

Since my anxiety and depression were often linked to my relationships, I decided to study that field, starting with John Gray's famous work, *Men are from Mars, Women are from Venus*. I liked his thesis until I learned more about him. It seems his ex-wife, Beverly DeAngelis, who wrote *Getting All the Love You Want*, is also a relationship counselor and they were married to each other before they became famous authors. Though their marriage ended bitterly and they reportedly still don't get along, they both went on to become relationship "experts." What the…?

While my cynicism grew, I read their books, listened to their tapes, bought their posters. Their messages were all the same: "Do what I say and you will be as happy, rich and good looking as I am."

And who is that man on TV who claims the answer to your happiness is to love your dear wife deeply and completely? He isn't even married, for Christ's sakes! How can he hold the answers?

I'd come to believe that truly happy people, like Rocket, do not feel the need to tell others how to live their lives. To me, the "experts" and gurus seemed too sure of their answers and too pious.

The one therapeutic avenue I didn't take seriously was talk-show psychobabble. I found it ludicrous.

Consider this quick story. A friend's daughter was attending college in Los Angeles. The student's boyfriend planned to move away, from LA to Salt Lake City, and pleaded with her to join him—and she wanted to—but the move would mean she'd have to change colleges and start over in the new city. Distressed, confused and seeking advice, my friend's daughter called a popular LA radio talk show psychologist, who self-righteously chastised her for putting a man in charge of her life and ordered the young woman to end the relationship, stay in school and become independent. My friend's daughter agreed and, before she hung up, she told the therapist how much help she had been. Then she moved to Salt Lake City. Still, this advice guru continues to use the taped conversation as a promotional ad for her show while she berates her callers about sexual abstinence and chastity (even though her own naked pictures ended up on the Internet as the result of what she called a "youthful indiscretion.")

My cynicism put on a bit more weight.

What are these people thinking? Do they really think a short confrontation on the radio or in front of a studio audience can really change a person's life? Eventually, I concluded that these people provide short-term coping strategies, at best. At worst, they do real emotional damage.

Today, when I encounter these people in the media or see their books on store shelves, I get angry that they aren't honest with people, because the fact is that *not one* therapist, so-called expert, self-help guru, book or religion ever told me the truth: that to feel better, I would have to work harder than I'd ever worked.

They can't *all* be naïve enough to believe their trademark brand of true happiness actually makes a difference in people's lives. Of all of the mental-health peddlers out there, at least one of them surely had the courage to say that the journey was terribly difficult, that the only way to get healthy was swim hard across waters so strong and dangerous that we would not have the strength left for the swim back.

But, no!

Difficult marriage? Attend a weekend workshop! Problems with your job? Find the color of your parachute! Chronic unhappiness? Just believe in your own personal power! Come on, you can do it! Just be like me! You don't have to look too deep. You don't have to do *really* hard work. Just change a few things—a nip here, a tuck there, a walk across burning coals—and...*Bingo!*

ess!

For a while, I bought their shtick. After all, I am American and self-help is a cultural phenomenon, an American obsession. We believe we can improve our lives through self-reflection and, thus, the psychology section of our bookstores always has the most customers and the most titles.

Don't get me wrong. Of course, I believe that we can work to make our lives happier and more fulfilling and I think that this is a noble quest. But, unfortunately, we Americans have come to expect our McCulture to apply to self-reflection—fast food Freud. We look for self-help programs that give us drive-through results. Willing to reflect on the sources of our unhappiness, we just don't want to look too deep, we don't want our reflection to make us too uncomfortable.

We Americans also tend to believe that we can *think* of a solution, that we are so smart and so innovative that we should *always* be capable of figuring out new solutions to old problems. This is what we do best! Americans are used to thinking that no problem is too big; if we just use our brains to analyze a situation—any situation—we will find the answers, achieve our goals and be happy.

It is not easy to accept that hard emotional work is the *only* path to significant change. I should know! I spent countless dollars, an incredible amount of time, and extraordinary effort seeking a "quick fix," always thinking that the next book, technique, philosophy or counselor would provide the quick fix to my emotional problems and help make me happy.

I'm not saying my search was fruitless. All my reading, watching, listening and thinking gave me an excellent intellectual understanding of the emotional process, and everything I learned helped, at least a little bit. But, finally, I realized that *the search itself was a manifestation of my own neurosis.* My rational analysis was an attempt at figuring out the answer to my anxiety and my life, but it allowed me to avoid the murky, ambiguous emotions that were bottled up inside me. Thus, it created more noise and helped me to avoid tackling the *real* dysfunctions I needed to confront. Of course, this realization was nothing new or original. All the great thinkers tell us the answer lies within us. I simply hadn't known what they meant.

Accustomed to thinking and persevering through tough issues, I always used hard work and determination to overcome adversities that included divorce, being fired from a good job, financial difficulties and raising two daughters. Through each crisis, I fought and scraped myself back onto my feet, so my best assets were my mind and my determination. When I set my mind to it, I was good at achieving things. In fact, I was so good at *doing* and *thinking* that I thought I could solve all my problems if I could figure out where they came from.

Why did it take me so long to let go?

My mind was the problem.

On a deep level, I was afraid of truly emotional work; as long as I engaged my mind in the process, I was able to avoid my feelings by covering them with the noise of thoughts. But it didn't work because depression and anxiety are *emotional* problems with *emotional* solutions.

Though we refer to therapy as "psychoanalysis," keep in mind that *analysis* of our problems is not the same as *dealing* with them. No matter how I approached my problems intellectually or analytically, I could only solve my emotional problems through deep and necessarily painful work. But, believing that I could overcome my unhappiness by analyzing and studying my problems—by *thinking* my way to happiness—I became frustrated and desperate. It wasn't working. While I was confusing deep intellectual understanding with deep emotional work, my intellectual quest for answers was fruitless and I was stuck.

It occurred to me that I never saw Rocket stuck. Sure, he had problems with his job and challenges with his kids, but he never seemed to worry like I did. He always seemed to believe that things would work themselves out. Rocket looked relaxed, even when there was something important on the line. When we played soccer together in college, whenever we had a critical kick or defensive play, he was always the one who stepped up. Rather than feeling the stress of big games, he seemed to enjoy pressure situations.

I envied him. I knew Rocket's easy nature had something to do with his parents, whom I met a couple of times. They didn't strike me as super parents—nothing special—but he never complained about them and genuinely seemed to like them. Rocket told me that his Dad gave him good advice, said his mom was "cool," and mentioned that both of them supported him in virtually everything he did.

While some emotional problems, like anxiety and depression, can have a genetic root, I wondered whether the opposite could be true: Could guys like Rocket be "hard-wired" for happiness? I didn't think so. Rather, I thought that his easygoing nature was probably a product of his relationship with his parents.

But I've heard the arguments that screwed up families—even those with an absent parent—can produce children who become healthy, well-adjusted adults and that some children who have healthy, supportive parents can emerge as seriously screwed up adults. Both sides of the coin are valid, legitimate. But the reality is that *most people with problems come from families with problems and most healthy people come from healthy, well-adjusted families.*

I would like to believe that my problems were genetic but, in reality, I was too afraid to look at my life honestly. On the outside, my life looked great, just like Rocket's—nice home, great kids, profitable business. But, in my case, it was a thin veneer. Just under the surface, I was teeming with chronic dissatisfaction, anxiety and unhappiness. To be honest, my life was in chaos.

At the time of my breakdown, my marriage was in shambles. I was burned out in my job but worked hard to make financial ends meet. I had trouble concentrating, felt nervous and found it difficult to sit still long enough to read the newspaper. Every night, I drank almost a bottle of wine—good wine, so it didn't seem tawdry. Since childhood, I'd had anxious behaviors—tweaks and tics, scratching and twitching—that grew worse as I neared my breakdown. I found relief in work. I used tasks, chores, and duties to avoid thinking. If I just kept *going* and kept *doing*, things wouldn't come apart and I wouldn't have to ponder my life, so I was exhausted and didn't realize it. Exhaustion—driving my mind and body so

I wouldn't have to think—was the only way that I could cope with my emotional pain. The fear of dealing with my problems kept me moving.

Suicide and other twisted thoughts pushed into my head. I was not depressed enough to act, but was terrified by the fact that I could even think about it, and the more I didn't want to think about it, the more I found myself thinking about it. That made me anxious. Even my *fear* of anxious feelings made me anxious and, in the end, I became anxious about the chance that I would become anxious. The anxiety grew extraordinarily painful as I began to ask myself if I *could* commit suicide.

I did not want to live the rest of my life in two worlds—simultaneously acting normal on the outside while freaking out on the inside. I needed relief, but I couldn't turn my mind off so I never got relief. Every day seemed like an eternity as I went to bed anxious and woke up anxious. Waking up in the morning, I looked forward to going to bed at the end of the day. But, when I did go to bed, I fidgeted and obsessed about my insomnia and feared the anxiety that I knew would be awaiting me in the morning. My only sleep came from sheer exhaustion. It was a living hell. It was torture.

Meanwhile, I looked great, wearing a mask of normalcy as I worked, parented and drank. Even when my second marriage ended, my best friends could not spot my looming breakdown.

And, then, everything fell apart.

One morning, a few weeks after the end of my second marriage and a week before Christmas, I woke up with the usual "buzz," shifting from horizontal anxiety to vertical anxiety. I pushed myself out of bed. I had to fly to San Jose for a meeting and I was bringing Maddy, my daughter from my second marriage, to visit Alexis, my daughter from my first marriage. Right about the time we went through airport security, my anxiety level was cresting. "I don't think I can do this," I muttered to myself like a Bizarro *Little Engine That Could*. "I don't think I can do this!" I made it through and we boarded the plane but, then, as the plane took off, I noticed a weird phenomenon: Everything seemed like a dream. The sunlight coming through the windows looked odd, filtered, like recent video of Cher. Everything seemed surreal. And, of course, it made me even more anxious. "I can't go crazy *now*," I told to myself. "I have *meetings* to attend!"

After landing, I got our bags, rented a car, buckled Maddy into her car seat and drove to my ex-wife's house. Alexis unbuckled Maddy from her car seat and the two of them ran into the house as I followed them. Alexis's mom, Diane, greeted me at the door. "Maddy," I said. "Come and say 'Hello' to Diane." Maddy ran over, Diane picked her up and I passed out.

Just for a second. Just long enough to terrify everyone, including me.

Diane drove me to the hospital where, we assumed, doctors would perform a quick evaluation, hand me some medications and release me. Diane dropped me off and agreed to look after Maddy until I came home. But the local emergency room was poorly equipped to handle me. The ER doc wanted to prescribe antidepressants and send me home, but I told him I'd tried most of them without much luck. During the conversation, I struggled to answer his questions. I couldn't think straight and had trouble talking. Picking up on my strange behavior, he decided to transfer me to the Santa Clara County Mental Health Center for evaluation—and I still thought I could make my meeting the next day!

I soon learned that a county mental health center is a poor environment to be in if you feel anxious or depressed. Sitting on a wooden bench in a windowless room, I waited to be evaluated. A guy in handcuffs, who was missing a large chunk of his nose, sat across from me making angry gurgling sounds. Finally, after about an hour, an orderly led me to another windowless room, where he told me that a psychiatrist would be along shortly to evaluate me.

Eventually, a short, rather anxious physician entered. He introduced himself and explained that his job was to diagnose my condition and recommend treatment options. He asked me questions from the Burns Depression Diagnosis Instrument.[3] A patient's answers to these questions indicate his or her level of depression. Of course, I was very familiar with the test from my reading. In fact, like a person obsessed with his or her blood pressure, I took the test often, checking my level of depression on a regular basis. However, being evaluated in the county psych unit, I didn't want to come off as depressed! It might have helped that I'd had so much practice with the text, except that I couldn't remember the "right" answers. My mind wouldn't cooperate.

After completing the test, the short, anxious doctor caught me off guard by asking an impromptu question: "How severe is your anxiety?"

Hey! I thought. *That's not fair! That question wasn't in the book!* He was diverting from my script! "Severe," I replied.

"On a scale of one to ten, ten being the most painful, how would you rate it today?" he probed.

"Nine point five," I said. I wanted to leave room for improvement.

"Do you ever think of suicide?" he queried.

That caught me off guard, too. How could I answer honestly without seeming depressed? At that moment, my depression felt like those times when I went to the dentist because of a toothache; it just didn't seem to hurt as much when I was sitting in the dentists' chair. "Not really *suicidal*, I wouldn't say," I answered. "But the anxiety gets so severe, sometimes I think if it doesn't go away I would rather be dead."

Wrong answer.

I wasn't going anywhere for a while.

The doctor took me back to the holding room and then the assistant escorted me back to the windowless room, while they called an ambulance to transport me to the local behavioral health center for observation. Waiting for an EMT to collect me, I couldn't believe it! Through all of my anxiety and depression, the one thing I feared the most was being labeled as crazy! I hid all my symptoms because I never wanted anyone to know how crazy my anxious fears sounded. And, now, my worst fear was coming true: I had been admitted to a psych ward.

All the times I worried and obsessed about going crazy and here I was! All my work, all my therapy, all my reading and searching led me to this place—a wooden bench, waiting to be transported to a psychiatric facility. Scraping bottom, I curled up on my bench, turned toward the wall and let go. I was crazy and I didn't care. It didn't matter what happened anymore. I just wanted relief.

Maybe I had a genetic/physiological/chemical imbalance brain imbalance. Maybe the only solution was medication. Maybe there weren't any answers, only more questions.

The EMTs strapped me to a gurney and wheeled me into the back of their ambulance for the drive from the Behavioral Health Center to the County Psychiatric Hospital Unit. One of the EMTs asked me to let him know if I had the urge to jump out the back of the ambulance. It was dark by the time we arrived at the psych unit.

The nurse told me that I would be staying there for at least five days. *Great way to spend Christmas,* I thought. But, actually, it was okay. I was tired—so *very* tired. I was tired from holding it together for so long, exhausted from acting normal, from doing my job, from lumbering forward carrying this incredible emotional burden. I was exhausted from presenting myself as fine when, behind the mask, I was an emotional basket case.

The anxiety and depression had won. More importantly, I didn't have to fight anymore.

What a day! I thought. I had started out in the first-class section of an airplane and ended up in a mental health hospital, lying in a single bed in a small, windowless room. A nurse told me that, if I wanted to shave in the morning, I would have to arrange for someone to bring me a razor and watch me. I guess if someone really wants to kill himself, even a disposable razor will work. That didn't make me feel any better.

Turning out the light, the nurse told me to stay in my room until someone came to get me in the morning. She locked the door from the outside. I heard someone groaning from the depths of a heavily drugged sleep. Desperate, frightened and alone in the dark, I pulled the blanket over my head and cried.

I needed help.

The Second Truth

You can't escape anxiety and depression on your own. You need help.

The first time I met Jane, I didn't like her. She was much more direct than my other counselors. Her probing questions made me uncomfortable; they were too, well...*direct.* She asked about my relationships, my jobs and my past. While I pretended that I was perfectly normal and strong in all of those areas of my life, the fact was that my relationships had no intimacy, I was burned out in my job, and my life was *not* healthy. Still, I reasoned, if I could *just* get rid of my anxiety, I would be fine. No need to open Pandora's box.

That was five years ago. My panic attacks were getting to me again and I was looking for a new counselor because I wasn't making much progress with the current one. That is, I wasn't experiencing any substantial relief from my symptoms and we seemed to be wasting time and money on a weekly basis. I thought a change of scenery might help.

Most of my past counselors had been easygoing, asking me questions like, "So, Steve, how do you feel about that? How does that make you feel?" Those are the sounds of a "supportive" counselor, which is great if you want support. But my anxiety just wouldn't go away and I was beginning to feel desperate. I wanted direction.

The referral service said Jane was a directive counselor; she gave more direction than support. Yep, that sounded like what I needed—someone who would tell me what to do. Or so I thought.

I had two sessions with Jane. The first was a get-acquainted meeting, the second more intense. She started probing deeper.

"Tell me a bit about your relationship with your wife," she said. "Would you say you are happy?"

Wait a minute. This was about my *anxiety,* not my relationships. Besides, what the hell did that question mean? Of course, I wasn't happy. My wife and I had been married for a couple of years and, like my previous relationships, our marriage was a constant struggle between neurotic dependence and bored aloofness. Wasn't that normal? "Of course I'm happy," I lied.

"Would you say you and your wife are intimate?" she asked.

"Well, sometimes sex is good," I replied. "But most of the time we just hang out, like roommates." This was a half-truth; we were entirely like roommates, as sex had become a thing of the past.

"No, no," she said. "Do you feel *connected* to your partner?"

"What, do you mean?" I asked. "Like *committed?*" It was obvious that I didn't get it.

She tried a different approach. "Would you say that you are in love with your wife?"

My reply was pure Steve McCourt. "I believe that love is a choice you make when you commit to another person," I declared.

"So, you feel more like friends than intimate lovers?" she continued probing.

"Of course," I said. "Doesn't everyone after a while? I mean, you have to really work at a relationship to stay in love, right? "

"Well, I guess I don't understand why you would stay in a relationship that is obviously devoid of intimacy," she said pointedly.

I didn't schedule a third appointment.

It would have been easy for me to dismiss Jane as too direct, too confrontational. But, to be honest, I wasn't ready to deal with the core issues of my unhappiness. Even if Jane had posed her questions in softer, gentler ways, I wouldn't have come back. I wasn't in enough pain.

Looking back, it's hard to believe that I wasn't in enough pain, since my anxiety was, at times, excruciating. It woke me up every day with an "anxiety buzz" that permeated the air around me. I could almost taste it. Each day was an exhausting struggle. First, I struggled to overcome anxiety that I couldn't possibly complete a given task without freaking out and then, as I began the task—whether it was to give a presentation to hundreds of top corporate officers, board an airplane, or do the laundry—I battled the anxiety of anticipating the *next* task. I never got a break; I was a perpetual anxiety machine! How did I put up with it? I labored just to make it through each day as I attended meetings and made presentations, spinning like a yo-yo from one side of the country to the other. Excruciating anxiety was my constant companion. Spending all my energy to cope with it, I wasn't even aware of whether I was enjoying my work. Why did I push myself so relentlessly? So that I would not have to examine my life.

Then there was the depression. My God, the depression! Difficult to put into words, it was an intense physical pain, like taking a cheese grater to my nerve endings. It was dark and bottomless. In the middle of a depressive episode, I felt that I would never, ever experience happiness again.

My depression and neurotic behaviors took their toll on me, emotionally and physically, and, of course, on my relationships. I was very alone. Determined to appear "normal," I couldn't let anyone know how much pain I was in, so I masked my feelings. No one suspected, not even my close friends or family and certainly not my co-workers. I could never let them find-out. If my family, friends or co-workers found out what was happening behind my mask, they might think I was crazy—and that might mean I *was* crazy!

By the end of each and every day, I was wrung out. Crawling into bed at night, I thought that I would find relief with sleep. But the anxious chatter in my head made real sleep impossible, as I lie in bed, obsessing about waking up the next day and performing it all over again. Deeply exhausted, I somehow found the strength each morning to get up and do it again.

I don't know how, but I hung on for years without falling apart. All the while, though, the costs of postponing my painful self-examination mounted. Of course, there was the cost in money, time and energy spent on books, therapists and my full-time searching process but, more importantly, there was the greater cost in years lost to unhappiness. I spent much too much of my life in loveless relationships that had dead-ended in the boring trudge of routine duty. I stayed with the women in my life long after the intimacy disappeared. But, I reasoned, it was better to be anxious and depressed *with* someone, rather than by yourself, right?

Despite the excruciating pain, coping seemed to be a better option than dealing with the core issues that made my life miserable. Opening up the many areas that needed work seemed like too huge an undertaking, too monumental a task. Where could I even *begin* to find the source of my emotional problems? Better to put up with crushing pain than to deal with my feelings.

While I knew, at some level, that confronting my deep, emotional demons was the only option, I wasn't yet ready to take on the project. I had not yet hit rock bottom.

Two years later, I did. I called Jane from the Santa Clara County Behavioral Health Unit. The doctors there refused to release me unless I produced a referral to a mental health professional. It seemed odd that I hadn't thought of Jane for two years but, when I was out of rope, when I hit the wall, she's the one who popped into my head. Although I'd seen other counselors in the interim without much success, somehow I knew that this probing, prying woman could help me.

My other counselors—Jungians, Freudians and cognitive-behaviorists—practiced the various therapeutic disciplines, which I understood because of my never-ending struggle to read my way to a cure. Jungians believe in archetypes, the collective unconsciousness of humans; this is great stuff, but this journey seemed too supernatural to relieve anxiety. Freudians said my anxiety originated in my Oedipal relationship with dear old Mom, but that explanation seemed too simplistic since it ignored all the other factors, like genetics and my maturation during the 25 years since I'd left home. It also placed too much blame on my mother. *What about Dad?* I thought. *Didn't he influence me, too?* I also saw cognitive behavioral counselors, whose approach benefited me the most. Dealing with the here and now—the present—they use a technique of identifying and then changing a patient's negative "voice." In other words, they challenged me to recognize the negative statements I recited to myself, and then worked to change them. This was the therapeutic equivalent of *The Little Engine That Could*: "I think I can! I think I can!" It's a very pragmatic approach.

My litany of therapists did not provide me with a cure, but their coping strategies helped me managed my anxiety. The problem for me was that cognitive behaviorism doesn't take into account the earlier influences in life, like upbringing and environment, so those counselors never led me to deal with the "core" issues of my unhappiness. This is probably why I liked them!

I also saw a psychiatrist who specialized in psychopharmacology, using medication as the primary treatment for emotional and psychiatric disorders. Due to the stigma attached to such medications, I hesitated to use any kind of anti-anxiety or anti-depressive drug. To my logic, it felt "weak" to rely on something other than my own mind to handle things. "I must be really crazy to need a drug (other than alcohol) to get through the day," I said to myself. The drug-specialist asked me a handful of questions and then prescribed different medications for anxiety and depression. The ten-minute consult cost me $120. Talk about a quick fix! But we never found a drug combination that "worked" for me. While the medications helped decrease my anxiety and made it easier for me to hold some of my feelings at bay, they also left me feeling unlike myself, and I never felt happy or cured from my anxiety. I was just sort of hanging on.

At times, I thought maybe I had set the bar too high. By my way of thinking, it wouldn't be enough to be free of anxiety; I wanted true happiness, without drugs. But I'd been searching for so long, I almost gave up on my hope for happiness, which seemed too far a distance to travel. By the time I ended up in the hospital, all I wanted was for the anxiety and depression to *stop*. *To hell with happiness!* I thought. I would have accepted boredom over the pain.

The other thing that dimmed my ambition for happiness was that I wasn't the only person who seemed unhappy. Many people in my life struggled to make it through the day, as most of my friends suffered from existential angst. They seemed to be *recovering from life*—not *living* it—so I grabbed on to the belief that being angst-ridden was *normal*. Searching for so long, I began to think that the *search* was *life*. *Maybe existential angst is the normal human condition,* I reasoned.

"Life is a struggle," one friend argued, summing it up. "And anyone who tells you different is either lying or ignorant."

"But don't you believe there are people who are truly happy?" I asked.

"Nope," he shook his head. "Only people who *think* they're happy. If they looked at their life honestly, they'd see how miserable they really are."

"You don't really believe that, do you?"

"Of course I do," he said. "Look at all the great writing and art that comes from the struggle." If Van Gogh had taken Prozac, my friend argued, he would have been a plumber. "What's the first noble truth of the Buddha?" he challenged me. "Life is difficult. Once you accept that, it makes it easier." The ultimate glass half-empty guy, he saw life as one long bout of existential angst.

But I couldn't buy into that belief system—because of Rocket. As far as I could tell, Rocket felt *no angst*. He was happy. He even played a different soccer game than I did. Always seeking out the most stressful position, he wanted the team to be able to rely on him. Confident without being arrogant, he was talented yet humble. And, though he made mistakes, he never obsessed over them. While I obsessed about my mistakes and all of life's stresses, Rocket seemed unaware of such concerns. He didn't pressure himself and, as a result, his life was foreign territory to me as he seemed content, fulfilled and relaxed.

According to my cynical friend, the only reason Rocket was so happy was because he was unconscious—unaware of his angst. If that was the truth, then I craved Rocket's unconsciousness; I wanted to drift through life without being nagged by anxiety of every minute of every day. But I knew Rocket and I knew that he *wasn't* unconscious. We had a deep and stimulating relationship with interesting conversations and intellectual exchanges that could not have occurred without conscious perception. So, while Rocket gave me hope for a cure, my counselors did not.

Most of my therapists believed that anxiety and depression were disorders to "manage"—not to cure. I once asked a counselor, "Do you believe a person can be cured of depression and anxiety?"

"Well," he replied. "I wouldn't say 'cured.' My goal is to give patients coping skills. With an effective and appropriate emotional toolbox, a patient can live a relatively happy life. You see," he elaborated, "most people have a genetic proclivity towards anxiety and depression. It is an endogenous condition. We are hard-wired for unhappiness."

Well, helping people to achieve "relative happiness" may be a noble calling to him, but it failed to give me much hope. Desperate for relief and desperate for happiness, hope was what I needed most. I faced the classic chicken-or-the-egg dilemma: How can a counselor, who doesn't believe anxiety and depression are curable, give a patient sufficient hope to begin the journey? If a therapist hasn't completed the journey himself, how could he possibly know the path to healing—or the reward for taking that journey? How can someone who hasn't experienced the difficulties of emotional work establish the trust to lead someone down that path? While such a therapist might *intellectually* understand the process, how would he know where to start if hadn't experienced it himself? To my mind, it was a problem that such a counselor didn't even believe in the existence of the egg—or the chicken...

My therapists also tried to reassure me with the genetic explanation. Once I told them my family history, they quickly became convinced that I was hard-wired for anxiety and depression. I almost fell for it. *Wouldn't it be easier,* I considered, *to find the magic medication that made me truly happy and take away these bad feelings?* Tempted to accept that my fate was genetic, I refused to go that route.

Why? Why didn't I give up? Why did I fight on, against the urging of my family and friends? I can't completely answer that. No one—not family, friends, or counselors—would have blamed me but, for some reason, I refused to accept that I could solve my problems by blaming them on my "endogenous condition." I think the reason behind it was my driven personality worked in my favor. Never one who could easily accept losing, I saw my journey as a battle—and, to me, quitting meant defeat.

So I would not be satisfied with "relative" happiness. I wanted—*needed*—true happiness. While my cynical friends had long since given up on it, I could not and would not. Then came Jane.

"How are you feeling?" she asked the first time I met with her after my hospital stay.

"Desperate and crazy," I replied.

"Let's start with 'desperate.' Why?" she asked.

"Because I don't feel like I will ever be happy," I whined. "If you knew all the energy I spent trying to feel better, you'd feel desperate too. All that work and I still ended up in a psych ward! Maybe I won't *ever* be happy. Maybe I should just find the right drug combination…"

"If you feel like medication might help then I can refer you to a psychiatrist who can prescribe something," she offered.

"What do you think?" I asked. "Can a person like me, who has had so much anxiety and depression over his entire life, ever be happy?"

"If you are willing to do the work," she said, "you can be."

"How can you be so sure?"

"Because I've seen it."

I wasn't going to take her word for it. "What do you mean, you've seen it?"

"I've had patients whose anxiety and depression was more severe than yours," she said. "And, after doing the work, they are living happy lives."

"*Relatively* happy?" I asked. "Or happy?"

"Happy," she said. "Not free from appropriate worry or concern, but happy. Not able to avoid sadness or grief altogether, but not obsessing over them, either."

Compared to my life of anxiety and depression, "appropriate worry and concern" sounded downright blissful! "You really believe I can be happy?" I asked. "Not depressed or anxious?"

"If you do the work, you can be happy," she said again, sounding confident, not arrogant. "Remember, you will never be free from concern or sadness but you *can* be happy. The work will be difficult and take time…"

I began to feel something I hadn't felt for a long time: hope. "How much time?"

"We don't know yet," she said. "I have to find out a bit more about you."

And that's how we began, with Jane's first gift—hope. Until then, I didn't realize how much I needed it. My lifelong ordeal had already drained me of any confidence that I could be happy and, while friends, family and counselors all urged me to accept my fate, Jane offered hope and, with it, the possibility of happiness.

Desperate and out of answers, I needed to trust someone who could take the reins and guide me. I was ready.

I learned that Jane only accepted those patients who were in enough pain—people like me, people who were ready. Not satisfied with people who poured out their problems week after week without tackling the real work necessary to change, she refused patients who weren't ready.

She told me that most therapists see two types of people: *clients* and *patients*. Clients pay the bills, showing up week after week to talk about their problems without wanting to work on real change. But *patients* work hard to understand and correct the patterns in their lives.

For a long time, I was a "client." I didn't really want to deal with the underlying causes of my unhappiness; I just wanted my anxiety to go away.

The first time I saw her, I wasn't ready. She knew that but I didn't. Then, when I was desperate—ready—and not one day sooner, I turned to Jane again.

While I was confused, disheartened, emotionally exhausted and cynical, Jane started slowly.

"How do you feel about using medication as a tool?" she asked me.

A tool? I thought. No one had ever referred to meds that way. *A crutch perhaps, but never as a tool.* "I don't really want to use medication if I can avoid it," I told her. "I've tried a lot of them and they mostly made me anxious."

"Well, some of the short-acting tranquilizers can take the edge off the anxiety," she said. "You may need something like that to be able to think clearly."

She was right. My mind was too tired to function properly. Intrusive thoughts and obsessions, which were signs of my mental exhaustion, tormented me. Trying relentlessly to hold down my feelings, my mind was spent. As a result, my emotions were raw. I reacted to loud noises and any sharp sound or movement caused me to "emotionally flinch." I felt as if I was walking out of the darkness, right into bright light. Like my eyes, my feelings were overly sensitive.

I decided to take her advice. I used Ativan—a cousin to Valium—for short-term relief when my anxiety grew overwhelming.

Jane employed an eclectic approach with me, incorporating aspects of various therapies that I had already tried. Dealing with the present, she made sure that I had coping strategies to get me through each day and she taught me to identify negative images and words that upset me. But she didn't leave it at that. Gradually, we began to confront my underlying unhappiness, my deeper issues and patterns. The more I came to trust her, the more I opened up.

"So, you say I can be happy, right?" I asked.

"No," she corrected me. "I said you will be happy if you do the work."

"How much work?" I asked, impatient and anxious. "How long will it take?"

"Well, how long have you felt anxious?"

"I had my first panic attack when I was about ten years old."

"Then we have a lot of work to do," she said. "At least a year. Maybe more."

A year? I was crestfallen. It seemed like a very long time. "You mean I won't feel better for a *year?*"

"No," she said, but she held her ground. "You should begin to feel better sooner than that, but the process will take at least a year. Maybe longer."

"Are you *sure?*" I asked. "Can't we speed it up? Shorten the process?"

"Steve, you have to understand that, because your panic and anxiety go so far back, we will have to address some childhood issues. That takes time."

I realized that this was different. Jane didn't offer any quick fixes or miracle cures, and she answered my questions with complete honesty, promising that if I did the work, she would be there to guide me. She never made a promise she couldn't keep. She knew that establishing trust meant being trustworthy. She never said I *would* be happy—only that, if I worked hard and embraced the process, I *could* be happy. No promises, no false hope. The results were always on me; as the professional, she would guide me and let me do the work.

In time, I began to see the power of a healthy patient-therapist relationship. With an unspoken agreement, we built a trusting relationship within solid, healthy boundaries. It was clear where our relationship began and ended for both of us—at the door to her office.

One time, I had a counselor who invited me to go on his boat with him. That seemed inappropriate and I felt that he'd stepped over a line. If that had happened earlier in my therapeutic history, I might have accepted his invitation but, as it was, I didn't schedule another appointment with him.

I knew another counselor who lived in a small town and who discussed his patients with friends, family and even acquaintances. His patients became conversation fodder at parties. That scared me. I wouldn't want anyone sharing the intimate details of my life as a form of entertainment.

Even today, when I think about some of my previous counselors, I get angry. So many seemed stuck, themselves. Though they might have had a good *intellectual* knowledge of the process, they seemed to have little (if any) firsthand understanding of the hard work it takes to see the process through. I wondered about their personal lives—whether they were normal and their relationships functional.

Indeed, some counselors were more neurotic than I was! Some used my vulnerability to prop up their own neuroses, trying to force me to see the things that they wanted me to see. One counselor, for example, told me to FedEx a letter to my parents to tell them not to contact me until further notice. I thought that this idea was both hurtful and unnecessary.

The fact is that it is extremely difficult for a person who is in serious emotional pain to be able to distinguish between qualified and unqualified counselors. I wasn't conscious of or informed about how to choose a therapist and I certainly did not have the good judgment or clear thinking that would help me know what to look for. Considering any patient's personal confusion, mental exhaustion and any other individual demons that might be at play, counselors and therapists carry the burden of a huge responsibility to be ethical, honest and self-aware.

Jane said she did her worst work when she tried to control the process. When she tried to "make" a patient see something—unconsciously projecting her own expectations—she actually interfered with her patient's progress. The fact that Jane recognized and controlled this tendency set her apart from the others.

I'm sure that many of Jane's patients gave up and went back to the comfort of old behaviors. I had certainly done that before! After my first marriage dissolved, I saw a counselor for a while and made some progress before I "fell in love." Then, since I felt *cured,* I didn't feel that I needed to see the counselor anymore. But, in fact, the truth was that I didn't have to deal with my emotions, because I had someone to deal with them for me!

At a point, I was tempted to repeat that pattern. My work with Jane was so emotionally and physically draining that I was tempted to find someone (another wife, perhaps?) or something (another drink, perhaps?) to distract me. But Jane knew when to hold up a mirror, to point out that I was deceiving myself. Not exactly tough, she was more direct and honest, and she knew when to apply pressure and when to back off.

"How much are you drinking?" she asked one session.

"Not much at all," I said, proud of my abstinence. "I have one glass of my favorite red wine in bed each night while I read."

"And you feel it doesn't interfere with our progress?"

"Well, before I used to drink at least a bottle of wine each night. Now a bottle lasts me three nights," I added proudly. "That's quite an improvement for me."

"Wait a minute. A bottle of wine holds four glasses of wine, not three. So shouldn't a bottle last you four nights?"

In bartender-speak, I was taking a "heavy pour." Jane held up the mirror and, after that, I stretched my bottles to four days.

"Sometimes," I told her during one early session, "I can't figure out where the feelings are coming from."

"What do you mean?" she asked.

"Well, sometimes I cry for no reason," I said. "It just pours out of me. Don't you think that's weird?" I was looking for reassurance.

"Your psyche knows where it's going," she said. "Just trust it."

"Yes, but it would be a lot easier if I could understand why I was crying. I'd feel better about it."

"Some of your feelings are pre-verbal, so naturally it's difficult to figure out where they come from."

"What do you mean, 'pre-verbal'?"

"Well, some of the times you got stuck happened when you were quite young," she explained, "before you could put those feelings into words. Children don't think like adults. They *feel*. They don't *think*."

"So, what do I do when these feelings start to overwhelm me?"

"It is important to stay with them, just to feel them," she said. "If they are too overwhelming, then use your Ativan. Eventually, you'll get comfortable with them."

I nodded.

"And," she continued, "you might feel better if you simply accept that the process is murky. We have to muddle through the feelings."

"Muddle through?" I asked. "Muddle through? I feel like I'm struggling just to stay sane. Isn't there any way to make it go faster?"

"The process will take as long as it takes and dig as deep as it has to dig."

"But I want to know where the feelings are coming from," I pleaded as my voice took on a whining edge. "Why do I find myself crying in the shower, in the car, in the airport? It can't be normal for a 45-year-old man to burst into tears for no reason!"

"It's normal if those feelings were repressed for 45 years," she said. "You are dealing with 45 years of suppressed grief and anger."

"But I feel so out of control," I said. "Like I'm going crazy."

"Steve, you are *not* going crazy," she reassured me. "You are doing incredibly difficult emotional work. You will be happy. Just hang in there."

Hang in there? *Hang in there! How?*

In the past, when I was coping with my emotional problems, I relied on my family for support, leaning on them through my problems with relationships, jobs or my children. But Jane helped me realize that the hardest part of the therapeutic process my family or friends could not help me with . My work had to be a solitary struggle. It was very lonely, and I felt that no one would understand it, except Jane.

Partly, this was because my anxiety and depression were rooted in my family life. My unhappy patterns established themselves when I was very young—when I was *in* the family dynamic. So, as much as I loved them, those people couldn't help me now.

In fact, they were part of the problem.

The Third Truth

In order to move past depression and anxiety, you must break with the family in which you grew up.

<hr>

"Your children are not yours.
They are the sons and daughters of life's longing for itself."

—Kahlil Gibran

My parents hadn't seen their granddaughter, Alexis, in almost a year, so I planned to take my daughter to Florida for a spring-break visit. Then, I was committed to the behavioral health center. The trip was coming up a couple of months after I was released and, despite all the drama in my life, I still felt I had to go. I hesitated to tell Jane about the trip because I thought she might question it. I was right.

"I'm going to visit my parents in Florida in two weeks."

"Is that a good idea?" Jane asked me.

"Well, we'd planned it for quite a while," I explained. "My folks are looking forward to seeing Alex. They only get to see her a couple times a year."

"But this is a very important time in your work," she argued. "I don't think seeing your parents will help you. In fact, it might hinder you."

"Well, it's only for a couple of days," I reasoned, realizing that, maybe, I was asking for permission. "And Alexis is really looking forward to it."

"Where will you be staying?" Jane asked.

"With them," I said. "They rented a two-bedroom place just so they would have room for visitors."

"I'm sorry," Jane insisted. "But that's *not* a good idea."

"Why not?" I asked.

"Let's just say that it may not be the healthiest thing for you right now. Can you find a hotel?"

"This close to the trip?" I argued. "I don't know. My folks will be very disappointed. My mom loves to cook for me. Is it really necessary?" I did *not* want to tell my mom that I was not staying with them, because I knew that such a discussion would not be pretty.

Jane pressed. "I'm going to ask you to trust me on this, okay?"

"It isn't that I don't trust you," I continued. "It's just that my mom will be so unhappy. She can be very persistent." An understatement.

"I'm sure you will work it out," Jane said.

I felt torn between two authorities. I didn't want to ignore Jane's request, but I did not want to hurt my mother's feelings, either. In the end, more compliant than committed, I went along with Jane. Finding a hotel room was easy, but it was *not* easy to break the news to my folks. That was the hard part. At first, my mother wouldn't hear of it but she gradually relented.

"Well, I don't see why you want to put yourself through the time and expense," she said, unhappy. "But, if you have to, then you have to." In the end, she seemed to let it go but I knew that she was hurt. True to her style, my Mom doesn't express herself directly but takes a roundabout route in her communications.

For example, on our first night in Florida, as we finished the main part of our meal, she asked me what I wanted for dessert.

"Nothing, Mom," I said. "I'm full. Dinner was great but I couldn't eat another thing. Thanks."

She emerged from the kitchen holding a plate with a wedge of pineapple upside-down cake. "Here," she pronounced, placing the slice of cake on the table in front of me. "I cut you a piece, just in case."

"Well, thanks, Mom," I said, feeling irked as I pushed the plate away. "But I said I'm not hungry."

"I guess I'll just have to eat it," she sighed. "How about you, Alex? Do you want a piece of cake?"

"No thanks, Grandma," Alex said. She was full, too.

Mom disappeared into the kitchen again and, a moment later, she walked out and placed a bowl of ice cream in front of Alex. "Here you go, Alex," she said. "I know you like ice cream."

Alex looked at me, confused about what to do or say.

"Mom!" I said, my anger shooting to the surface as I almost shouted. "Didn't you hear what she said? She doesn't *want* dessert!"

"I was just trying to help," she said, as if she was the one who was put out.

"You don't want any dessert," she whined. "You don't want to stay with us…I guess you just don't need *anyone* anymore, do you?" My mother had no idea that she had gone too far.

An uncomfortable, unfamiliar feeling pushed its way to the front of my mouth. It was *rage*. My mom's persistence triggered a frightening amount of anger in me. It caught me off guard. I could barely contain it."That's *it!*" I said. "Put your coat on, Alex. We're *going!*"

Leaving my parents in a state of shock and incomprehension, I was irate, furious. I almost broke off the key as I stuck it into the ignition of the rental car. By the time we got back to the hotel, I calmed down. Alex changed into her pajamas and switched on the television, while I went into the bathroom to brush my teeth. Something strange happened.

Every time I put the toothbrush into my mouth, I gagged, and my face flushed as if I had a fever. Dizzy, I plopped down on the edge of the toilet. Then a huge—and I mean *huge*—wave of exhaustion plowed into my chest. I couldn't catch my breath. It wasn't a panic attack or a heart attack, but an exhausting heaviness. Then, suddenly, grief swept over me.

I convulsed into uncontrollable, wrenching sobs, crying until my throat ached and my sides cramped.

Scared and confused, I grabbed my cell phone, retreated to the seclusion of the bathroom and called Jane. I got her answering machine, left an emergency message and waited, barely hanging on.

"I got your message," she said when she called a few minutes later. Her tone was comforting, as if she was expecting my call. "Tell me what's happening."

I described the evening to her and told her about all of my symptoms.

"These feelings are perfectly natural," she said confidently.

"Not to me," I said. "It feels like I'm sick or something. It feels *physical*, not mental."

"Those are the pre-verbal feelings we talked about," she explained. "They can be very intense."

"*Intense?*" I questioned her. "These are *more* than intense. I can't control them!"

"Steve, these feelings go far back into your childhood," she explained, "back to when you got stuck and you didn't have words to describe them. But they are magnified by all the years you held them down."

"It feels like I'm going crazy," I continued. "I am so out of control."

"You're *not* going crazy," she reassured me. "Many patients share the same experience that you're describing, and they got through it. So will you. The feelings *feel* out of control only because you've held them down for so long. Do you have your medication with you?"

"Yes."

"This might be a good time to take something," she said. "Steve, I want you to remember two things. Can you do that?"

"Maybe." I said, though I felt like I was incapable of remembering anything.

"Okay," she continued. "First, you are *not* going crazy and, second, this is work you have to do, but *not* all at once. Use your medication when you feel overwhelmed. The feelings are intense but you will feel better. Understand?"

"When?" I said, pleading. "When will I feel better?"

"Be patient," she said. "And remember your medication. You're doing great work. I'll see you when you get back to Seattle."

That night was full of interesting dynamics because it was the beginning of a process for me: the two-year process of my growing up. My refusal to stay with them on that vacation was the first adult boundary I had ever set with my parents. It was my first, tentative step in my separation process—the process of breaking with my family and escaping the legacy of anxiety and depression–as I declared my independence and my right to adulthood.

Though I was still their son, I could no longer be their child. I was leaving home. Of course it would cause grief and stress; it was unnatural to think it wouldn't. Leaving parents behind—I mean, *really* leaving them behind—is hard enough for teenagers, but the bonds of a 45-year-old are knottier and tougher to break. In the same way that chicken pox and some other childhood diseases are more dangerous to adults, so the appropriate passages of youth are harder for grownups to endure.

Jane assured me that my break with my parents was normal and natural—a part of being human—and, more, that it was essential to becoming an independent, healthy adult. Without processing these feelings, without incorporating them into who I was, I couldn't begin to separate, grow and become *adult*. But breaking away made me feel like a 45-year-old teenager, an irrational adolescent in a middle-aged body.

Teenagers set boundaries with their parents. They grow more private, cutting off their parents from the more personal parts of their lives. But I hadn't done that when I was a teenager. I put it off until after my mental breakdown, until my therapy with Jane, until that trip to Florida.

But that was just the first of many more opportunities I would have to break away from my parents. While my mother tried to mother me and my Dad tried to treat me like the child I had always been, I could no longer put up with it. I couldn't let it go. Their irritations found an open wound as I suddenly had to stand up for my right to become an adult.

In the next six months, raw feelings often overwhelmed me. Every time I set a boundary, it triggered grief—natural and normal grief. I mourned a very important part of my life: my childhood. Smashing the mirror of my youth and cutting myself off from the comforting, comfortable embrace of my parents, I did not anticipate how difficult it would be, for I didn't realize the strength of my attachment to the soft pillow that my parents represented.

"I would have preferred if we'd had an opportunity to process those feelings here, in my office," Jane said when I returned from my trip.

"You mean, instead of on a bathroom floor in Florida?" I said sarcastically.

"Yes," she said. "When you insisted on taking that trip, I debated with myself how direct to be with you. It is such a delicate time in your therapy."

"Maybe it would have been easier if I'd stayed with them," I wondered.

"I don't think so," she argued. "It might have been worse. At least, at the hotel, you had some distance and privacy where you could deal with your feelings."

"My anger freaked me out," I said. "All week long, they just pushed my buttons. Yeah, it would have been worse if I had stayed with them."

"How was Alex through all of this?" Jane asked.

"I told her I was having a tough time," I said. "She told me she didn't understand but said she probably would when she gets older."

"Smart kid."

"Yes, she is," I smiled. "The highlight of her trip was meeting Ken Griffey, Jr, the baseball player. He was staying in our hotel. Alex will remember meeting him before she remembers her dad having a rough time."

"I'm sure you're right," Jane said.

Thus, the process began. It would take me a long time to be comfortable with those feelings but, over time and very slowly, I did become comfortable and even protective of my feelings, especially my grief. Meanwhile, all the people who cared about me wanted to make me feel better and tried to cajole me into being my old self: cheerful, at least on the surface. But I wanted to honor my feelings and I wanted the privacy to explore them, especially my grief. My difficult feelings seemed to become less powerful if I shared them with others, except for Jane. As a result, I stopped discussing my personal life with my family, especially with my dad. I no longer wanted either of my parents to have visibility into my personal life.

I also felt as if I had created my feelings and I wanted to deal with them. To feel independent, I needed space. That meant that I did not want to let Mom and Dad mother and father me. Through this process, little issues—magnified by the intensity of my emotions—loomed absurdly large. Like a teenager who wants to feel grown up, I did not want my mom doing my laundry when she visited, and I continued to stay in a hotel when I visited them unless I limited my stay to one night.

My needs for privacy and independence merged as I confronted my parents when they tried to make me feel guilty about my life and my choices. In spite of two failed marriages and having been fired from a job, I was proud of my life and proud that I never gave up. What's more, I was doing hard work and had determined that no one had the right to make me feel ashamed of myself.

Sounds like a teenager, doesn't it? Just like an adolescent, I was self-absorbed and unsure of the rules. Groping forward in the dark towards true adulthood, I made mistakes. I said things that I wanted to take back. I forgot to call and missed birthdays and anniversaries.

I heard through the family grapevine that Mom was hurt because I didn't stay at their house anymore and Dad was confused because we weren't "buddies" anymore. Their "child" was growing up. Though we were going through a temporary, necessary step in separating and maturing, it was hard on all of us, but Jane assured me that I would reach a point when my feelings wouldn't be so intense. I had to trust her and the process.

"Boy," I told her. "I'm having a tough time with Mom."

"She's probably having a tough time with you, too," she said.

"She keeps holding on to the old patterns," I said. "She wants to have the 'old Steve' back."

"It is tough letting go," she replied. "But it's necessary for both of you."

"But it seems so unfair," I said. "She doesn't understand. And Dad doesn't show it but I know he's wondering what is going on, too."

"Hang in there," she advised. "It'll get better."

"I think the relationship we had in the past is over," I said. "I don't think I can ever let them treat me like a child again."

"I hope not," she said. "You *aren't* a child anymore. How old do you *feel?*" she asked with emphasis.

I thought about it. "That's a funny question," I said. "I don't know. Maybe 15 or 16. Yeah, that sounds about right."

"Steve, that's progress," she said. "The relationship you had with your parents is over, because it *had* to come to an end. But, trust me, you *will* experience a new, more mature and perhaps deeper relationship, if they will let you. It will take time and work, but it can happen."

"How long will it take?" I asked, though I should have known better.

Jane just gave me a sarcastic smile.

"I know! I know," I chimed in. "It will take as long as it takes," I parroted. "But, if I do the work, it will happen."

"You're getting the hang of this!" Jane laughed.

My parents and I were not the only ones who were struggling. My siblings were too. I wished that they understood what I was going through and thought about trying to explain it to them. I raised the idea with Jane.

"Why do you want to discuss it with them?" she asked, discouraging me.

"Well, they seem so confused and upset," I explained. "I'd like to help them out by explaining where I'm coming from."

"This is a very important question so give it some thought," she suggested. "Do you think either your mom or dad went through this process with *their* parents?"

"No," I said, instantly. "Definitely not!"

"You sound pretty confident," she observed. "What makes you so sure?"

"Well, neither of my parents ever lived alone," I explained. "They went straight from high school and living at home to marriage and kids."

"Yes, but couldn't they still have done this type of work?"

"No way," I said. "I've seen them with their parents. They still have a parent-child relationship."

"What makes you so sure?"

"I just know it," I said. "In my bones."

"Well, then," she said, "it isn't a good idea to bring it up. It wouldn't be safe."

I let it go, for the time being, but I knew that we would revisit the issue. Still, I have to give my parents some credit. They could have made it much worse for me. While they didn't understand my behavior, slowly—*very slowly*—they did begin to accept my new rules and my adolescent behavior, and they did let go.

In the process, I began to feel both empowered and scared. Smashing the foundation of familial support that I'd taken for granted all my life, I realized I had no one to rely on but myself. What if I got sick? Who would take care of me? What if I lost my job? Where would I live? Cutting myself off from Mom and Dad, I was not only ending the relationship as we knew it but also forcing myself to be more independent and self-reliant. My God, I really *was* a teenager!

Just about then, my Dad surprised me.

Every summer, my family gathers for a reunion at the Jersey Shore, renting a large house that could accommodate everyone. That year, the house was bigger than the crowd and we had extra bedrooms. My 26-year-old nephew was coming with his girlfriend but, when my dad found out, his reaction was predictable. "It's okay to for her to come," he told my sister and her husband. "But she won't be staying under my roof. You'll have to find a hotel where she can stay."

Unfortunately, Dad said this in front of me and, at the time, I was practicing amateur boundary-setting. Though my sister agreed, planning to spend the afternoon searching out a hotel, it seemed stupid to me.

"Wait a minute!" I protested. "This girl is traveling all the way from the Midwest with Jeff? Why can't we can make an exception and give her the extra bedroom?"

My sister and her husband shot me a dirty look as if to say, "Don't start any trouble."

But, like a self-absorbed teenager, I was undeterred. "I think we should make her feel welcome," I continued.

Dad wasn't giving in without a fight. "You live under my *roof*, you live by *my* rules," he countered.

"But this *isn't* your roof," I argued. "We all split the rental fee, so it's *our* house."

"I paid the security deposit," he snapped back. "That makes *me* the one in charge!"

"*We* make the arrangements for the house every summer," Mom chimed in, attacking my left flank. "And don't talk to your father like that."

I couldn't fight a war on two fronts and decided to concentrate all my forces on my father. "Mom," I said, "this is between Dad and me. Stay out of it." *Wow!* I thought. *Did I really say that?*

My mother registered a look of hurt and anger as she backed off.

I went on the attack. "Well," I said, turning to my father, "if you tell me the amount of the security deposit, I'll pay half, because I think we should make this girl feel welcome. For Christ's sake, we *have* the extra room!" I felt extremely shaky challenging the head of the pack so recklessly, but I was in argumentative mode and I looked confident. Dad saw that I wasn't backing down.

"Well, okay, Mister Smart Guy," he said. "She can stay with us but *you're* responsible for guaranteeing that they don't sleep together. If they do, I'm going to hold you *personally* responsible."

I agreed. Leaving the room, I felt wobbly and yet stronger and more confident as I had demanded to be regarded as an adult. I was fighting a war to grow up—and I was going to win it. I had to.

But I have to give my father credit, too. On the last day of our vacation, I was packing the car when he wandered over and sat down on the steps. "I want to thank you for something," he said.

"Oh, yeah?" I said. "What's that?" I felt a little suspicious of his intention.

"For stopping me the other day about Jeff's girlfriend."

"Well, it worked out well, didn't it?" I asked him.

"Yes," he said. "But I appreciate your taking the reins, if you will."

I felt slightly uncomfortable. "Maybe that's where I get my stubbornness," I said, with a friendly smile.

"You know, Stephen," he said. "I get tired sometimes, making all the rules, being the enforcer. It's time someone else took over. So I wanted to thank you for that."

I was stunned and touched. This was *not* like my father! "You're welcome," I stammered.

At that precise moment, I realized that we would never be close in the same way again and I felt sad to be leaving that part of our relationship behind. A difficult, controlling and aloof Man, my dad also cared for me the best he could, giving me a good education, feeding his ten children on a professor's salary, and allowing me to make many of my own decisions. What's more, he is a good man.

Having confronted him, I fought guilt for that and for denying him access to a part of myself, but I knew that I could no longer allow him to treat me like a child. Sad that growing up meant I had to leave behind the closeness that we had shared, I knew that part of my life was over, and this triggered more grief.

Eventually, I heard through the McCourt grapevine that my siblings were unhappy with the new me. Typical of my family, they were uncomfortable with confrontation. "Everyone's wondering why you and Mom aren't getting along," one brother told me. A sister said, "Everyone's wondering why you have to be so confrontational with Mom and Dad." Another said, "You know, Mom's very upset you didn't stay with her in Florida." And then came the clincher from yet another sibling: "Everyone wants to know why you can't just let things go. You should realize that they're too *old* to change."

"This isn't about *them* changing," I told them. "It's about *me* changing. I don't really care or expect Mom or Dad to change." That was the truth. It was not about my parents, but about getting myself to the surface so I could breathe fresh air. If only they could understand that I didn't *want* to break with my family, but I *had* to.

I knew they loved me and I knew that my behaviors confused them; my Mom and Dad couldn't understand, and neither could my siblings, but the fact was that, to break the old patterns, I had to rely on myself.

"How could I possibly be on the right track," I asked Jane, "when everyone in my family—and I mean *everyone*—thinks I'm nuts?"

"You're not nuts," she told me. "You are doing great work."

"But they all want me to leave my folks alone, let things go," I complained. "They say my parents are too old to change! Christ, they sound like a bunch of Mooney's!"

"Don't listen to them," Jane advised. "They'll get used to it. Just keep doing what you're doing And listen to what your heart tells you to do."

Something clicked. Listen to my heart. This was new. "Yeah, my heart…" I said. "My heart isn't telling me to go back to the old patterns. My heart tells me to keep going!"

Deep down, I knew that I was on my own, that no one could help me or understand me because I was on my own journey, grappling with *my* life and *my* happiness. But their defensiveness made sense as well. After all, weren't they also losing a brother?

"You do understand what is going on, don't you?" Jane asked.

"Not really," I said. "I see some things, but not the whole picture."

She offered to explain some other aspects of the situation. "The patterns that make you unhappy," she said, "became part of you at a very young age, when you were a child. You have replicated those patterns in your life—in your failed marriages, your jobs, even your friendships."

"Can't you just point them out to me?" I smiled. "That would help a lot!"

"I can see *some* of them, but I can't understand how they affect you," she explained. "Some of your family patterns affect you more than others and I don't know why. That's work *you* have to do."

"But why do I have to break with my family?"

"You need some emotional distance to see how much the patterns define you and your life," she continued. "When you are *in* the pattern, you can't *see* it."

"So I need some objectivity, some distance?"

"I'm afraid so, Steve. This is something your family can't help you with, because they might even interfere with the process."

While I was going through a transition that I never made as a young man, the process of breaking free caused me intense pain. Whenever I set boundaries, my grief rose up. Whenever my parents or siblings held on to past behaviors, it triggered intense anger in me, though the anger sometimes made it easier because I learned to use it as a tool for setting boundaries and it helped me to overcome the guilt of cutting them out of my life.

Still, by necessity, my journey was a lonely one. Dealing with my grief made me understand the difference between being lonely and being alone. Like a teenager needs space, I needed to insulate myself from my family. I *needed* to be alone, needed to grapple with my feelings in private, in order to break with my family. But I did not expect the loneliness.

"I feel very alone," I told Jane.

"Tell me more about that."

"I remember the first Christmas I spent on my own," I said. "I was living in an apartment near college and didn't have the traditional family Christmas. It is the same feeling—very alone."

"You *are* alone," she said.

"I guess so," I frowned. "And that makes me sad."

"You may not be able to see it yet but there's also a strength that comes from relying on yourself, an empowerment."

"Maybe," I said. "But I can't see past that right now."

"I know. It's a very lonely place," she nodded. "But trust me. You'll feel better having gone through this."

"I hope so."

The session ended. I paid Jane and walked out to my car, feeling so lonely. It was as if everything was tinged with sadness. But, at some core, unspoken level, I knew that she was right, so I placed my trust in her and accepted my fate. It didn't make me feel any better, but at least I knew intuitively that what I was doing was necessary.

I got divorced from my second wife after my stint in the hospital so I was newly divorced when I went through my lonely therapeutic journey. I think that made it tougher, although it likely would have been difficult for a partner to cope with what I was going through, especially if the problems I was dealing with revealed some of the patterns of our relationship. Oh well. Jane pretty much assumed my marriage, which was devoid of intimacy, tenderness and empathy, was over anyway. So we forged ahead.

The philosopher George Satanaya said, "Those who do not remember the past are condemned to repeat it." I agree with that, but it's easier said than done! While I vividly remembered my past, I continued to repeat it. I couldn't break my patterns of unfulfilling relationships and unhappiness simply by understanding them through therapy, because my patterns were *emotional*, not intellectual. That's why I couldn't significantly change my future with self-help books or religion. Only emotional work would reveal and finally crack the patterns and only emotional work would allow me to break free of them.

Recently, I got a phone call from Patricia, a close friend from college. "Steve," she said, sounding pained and upset. "I need help."

"Patricia?" I asked. "Where are you?"

"In the bathroom at my parents' house," she said through her tears. "They won't leave me alone."

It was déjà vu for me.

"They keep telling me what to do with my life," she said. "And when I tell them they're making me feel bad, they say they are just trying to help. What should I do?"

"Are you ready to hear what I'm going to say?" I asked.

"I think so," she said cautiously.

"You need to get out of that house and find somewhere else to stay," I advised her. "Right now!"

"I can't do that," she said, almost pleading. "They fixed up my old bedroom for me. It would upset them too much..."

"Patricia, it isn't safe to expose your feelings to them," I insisted. "It won't help. Get out and worry about them later. Take care of yourself!"

An hour later, she called me from the hotel, distraught, as the episode had triggered incredible grief in her. As we talked about her experience, she slowly calmed down. At the beginning of her process, Patricia has yet to do the work necessary to break free and, though it is scary and painful, she *will* reach the other side if she stays focused and does the work.

The thing is that, at some point, the parenting that served us so well as children no longer works. Instead, it inhibits growth. To move forward, both parent *and* child need to let go. But, because I'd put it off for so long, "letting go" was more like tearing a membrane: It caused me tremendous agony that night in Florida. Tearing away from the warmth and comfort of my family left a painful, empty void in me as it stirred up feelings I'd kept under wraps for a very long time. It was terrifying. And, even though I thought I had those feelings under control...

I actually didn't.

The Fourth Truth

You are not in control of the healing process. The more you try to control the process, the longer it takes to reach the other side.

"If you do not bring forth what is within you, what you do not bring forth will destroy you."
—The Gnostic Gospel of Thomas

When I was 35, my panic attacks resurfaced with a vengeance. I'd recently been fired from one job and was starting a new job, while my marriage was coming apart. We were moving from California to Seattle, selling one house and buying another. While I was going through all these major life events, I didn't feel *anything*—not even stress. Then, it happened.

I was in a meeting with my new boss when, out of nowhere, I started blushing. Every time my boss looked my way, I turned beet-red. I became extremely self-conscious, fearing that she would notice my peculiar behavior, think something was wrong with me, and reconsider her hiring decision. With little success, I tried to control my blushing but the more self-conscious I grew, the more I felt my face reddening. Struggling to pay attention to my new boss, I was trying to control my blush response at the same time and, as a result, my anxiety spiraled. I suddenly thought I might faint. The walls closed in and my vision started to blur. I excused myself, blurting out something about indigestion, and drove to the emergency room. I didn't understand what was going on and wanted to convince myself that it was something I ate—something physical, something simple—*anything* but mental!

With chest pain, labored breathing and excruciating pain, my anxiety came crashing down. Though I thought I was dying, I feared a heart attack less than my loss of control. I could take the pain. I could handle gasping for breath and even the incredible anxiety, but I could not endure the thought of *losing it*. Of all my fears, losing my job, my family and everything I'd built was not my worst fear. Losing control was the worst. For my entire life, I'd held my emotions in check and, now, I couldn't master them. It was my definition of *hell*.

The ER doctor wanted to prescribe me something to calm my nerves. But, God forbid I should find some relief with drugs! That would be admitting that I was out of control—that I couldn't handle it myself—and I wasn't going to let that happen. I had a new job, a wife and a new house, and we were moving, for Christ's' sake! I couldn't fall apart *now*! I swallowed my pride and some medications.

With help from the pills, a couple of sessions with a shrink and my rededication to a dead relationship, I pulled my life back together. I wasn't happy, but I had dodged a bullet. At least, that's what I thought.

For the next ten years, I continued to stuff my emotions though, during that time, one marriage ended and another commenced. I had two children, wrote books and built a lucrative consulting practice, though I couldn't have done any of it without self-medicating with alcohol, engaging in chronic therapy and employing avoidance behaviors like sex, work and lots of golf. By the time I finally began to work with Jane, I'd stifled and stored up my emotions—including my accompanying anxiety—for ten years. I had a lot to deal with.

"Let's talk a bit about growing up," began Jane. "Okay with you?"

"Sure," I said. "What do you want to know?"

"Tell me about your parents. How was your relationship with them as a child?"

"To tell the truth I really don't remember much about them," I said. "I mean, with nine brothers and sisters, they were pretty busy."

"Did you feel they were there for you?"

"What do you mean, 'there for me'?"

"Did you feel your parents were there for you when you were upset or sad?" she probed.

"We are Catholic," I said. "We weren't allowed to be sad." When I was a child, crying was not an option. Whenever I fell down and scraped my knee, my parents told me to offer it up as a penance. "Rub it," Dad always said without empathy. "You'll be fine!"

I remember crying in the front seat of the car as my mother drove me to the dentist to remove a badly decaying tooth. "Why are you crying?" she asked me.

"I'm scared," I explained. "He's going to give me a needle."

"Needles don't hurt," Mom said.

"Yes, they do," I claimed. "The flu shots we get hurt bad."

"You're being a baby," she said. "Jesus didn't cry."

"What?"

"Jesus didn't cry when he was crucified," said my mom. "The Centurions nailed him to the cross and he didn't make a sound."

I stared out the window.

"If Jesus could stand having nails driven through his hands and feet without even a tear," she argued, "you should be able to bear a little needle. Just think about Jesus and offer it up."

She neglected to mention that Jesus was in his thirties at the time and, besides, he was the Son of God! That's a pretty high bar for a ten year old.

When I was 18, my very first girlfriend dumped me. Devastated, I moped around the house for weeks while my parents told me to forget her. "There are lots of other fish in the sea!" they said, trying to cheer me up. "You're better than her, anyway."

We weren't allowed to get angry, either. Only adults could get angry. So, while Dad and Mom grew angry from time to time, they reprimanded us kids if we showed our tempers. They reasoned that, if a person had a good reason to hurt me or make me mad, I had no right to get angry in response. So everyone else's reasons were justified, even if they were being cruel. By their thinking, no one ever did anything "on purpose," no one *intended* to hurt or disappoint me. Since everyone did "the best they could," their intentions were good and, therefore, my anger was never justified.

One time, Jay, a kid up the street, set our backyard swings on fire. When I cried to my mom, she said it wasn't Jay's fault. "His parents both work," she told me, "so he doesn't get the attention he needs. He just has too much time on his hands."

Naturally, I stuffed my anger, and then I felt guilty for getting upset. In time, people could do *anything* to me and I refused to allow myself to get angry.

"So, what did you do with all those feelings?" Jane asked.

"What feelings?"

"The sadness you felt toward your parents when they weren't around," she said. "The anger you felt about Jay setting your swings on fire. And the anxiety about going to the dentist."

"You think I was angry?" I asked. "I didn't *feel* angry."

"I think you have a lot of feelings inside from your youth," Jane said. "Do you ever feel sad that your parents weren't there for you as a child?"

"You think I'm *angry* at my parents?" I asked, avoiding the question.

"I don't know," she said. "*Are* you?"

"Do you think this has something to do with my anxiety?" I asked.

"Those feelings are coming from *somewhere*," she said. "Maybe it's a good place to start. What did you do with all those feelings?"

"Stuffed them, I guess."

"But you just can't 'stuff' feelings," she pointed out. "They don't vanish into thin air. They have to go somewhere."

"I don't know," I said. "I just didn't feel them. They went away, I think."

Jane stopped me. "Wait. Wait," she said. "Feelings don't go way, either. If they don't have an outlet, they build up, inside."

Most of my life I suppressed my "negative" emotions—sadness, fear and anger—because I was taught that such feelings were "inappropriate." Since nothing was painful enough to cry about and no anger was ever justified, I stuffed these emotions.

Where did they go? I had never thought about that. I also never considered that, at some point, the pressure would be stronger than my control, that at some point the feelings would start to "leak out."

"You said your father suffers from psoriasis and nervous tics," Jane said. "And some of your siblings do, too?"

"Yeah."

"I think you should look at that," Jane suggested.

I always believed that being nervous, fidgety and impulsive were just typical teenage behaviors. I still think so. But, when such behaviors continue into a person's forties, maybe it's time to take another look.

My mom had a name for my fidgety behavior: "St. Vitus's Dance." A Catholic priest from the Middle Ages, St. Vitus had a nervous disease that left him unable to hold still, so Catholics named a dance step after him. I must have contracted the same disease.

In grade school, the nuns complained that I couldn't sit still and had no self-control. My poor concentration and jitteriness ruined my penmanship and, one day, Sister Alma Dolores, who was a bully, called me out of class to discuss my low handwriting grade.

"Your mother called me last night to talk about your penmanship, young man," she scolded me.

"She did?" My upbringing did not allow me to consider the possibility that she might be lying.

"Yes," said Sister. "She is very hurt that you don't love her."

"But I do love her," I said, confused.

"If you really loved her, your handwriting would be better," she continued. "Why would you do that to your mother, young man?"

"Do *what*?" I asked, feeling even more confused.

"Why would you hurt her with your poor handwriting?" she said. "If you do not improve, your marks on your next report card are going to be low. Now, you don't want to hurt your mother when she sees your poor grade, do you? Think about that, young man!" With that, she waved me back into the classroom.

Though Sister Alma must have thought that this little talk might serve to motivate me to improve my handwriting, all it did was motivate me to avoid nuns for the rest of my life!

"Why weren't you allowed to get angry?" Jane asked. "Can you talk about that? I'd like to understand that better."

"Whenever any of us got angry," I started, "my Mom or Dad made excuses to defend the person who'd made us feel that way. Always. They'd say that the kid's parents weren't around much, or they didn't have two parents, or bring up some other reason to explain their behavior."

"What has one got to do with the other?" Jane asked.

"What?" I asked, puzzlement on my face. "What do you mean?"

"Well, even if a person has a good reason, that doesn't make it wrong for you to get angry," Jane explained. "Your feelings aren't connected to someone else's upbringing or situation. They're just your feelings."

"So, you're saying that, even if a person has a reason for doing something to me, I still have a right to get angry?" I asked.

"Yes," Jane nodded. "You have a right to be angry, regardless of another person's reasons or circumstances. One has *nothing* to do with the other. They are not connected."

"Wait a minute," I said. "You're saying I have a right to be angry with whomever I want? Regardless of the reason?"

"You have a right to feel whatever you feel whenever you feel it," she said. "They're *your* feelings."

"But, then…What about my parents?"

"What about them?" Jane echoed.

"I remember being very upset with my Dad because he wasn't around when I was young," I said. "I could never get his attention. But he worked two jobs and had ten kids, so his intentions were good and there were good reasons why he wasn't around."

"*Intentions* don't mean anything to a young child," Jane explained. "Children don't understand reasons or excuses. They just want their parents around. When kids don't get the love and attention they need, they feel sad and angry."

My eyes brimmed with tears—the tears of a ten year old. "But they were busy with all the kids and work and…"

"Stay with the ten year old, Steve," she coached me. "Ten-year-old children do not care about reasons or excuses or explanations. They just want love."

"It was very painful," I said through tears. "When I see myself as that little boy, in so much pain and anxiety, I feel incredibly sad."

"That's the grief you didn't feel as a child," Jane said. "That is an incredibly painful scene for any child, but you went through it alone, with no one to comfort you…"

"But they meant well," I argued. "They were doing the best they could."

"Yes," Jane nodded. "They had good reasons, but good reasons mean nothing to a child."

On my own between sessions, I was in agony as the child inside my heart was fighting with the adult in my head. Grieving for the pain that I suffered as a little boy—alone, anxious and struggling to cope without the love I desperately sought—I struggled with my rational, adult understanding: My parents truly did the best they could; they had good reasons for raising me the way they did. Since I comprehended those reasons, it didn't seem fair for me to be mad at them. But could I understand them as an adult and still be angry with them as a child?

I was still grappling with this concept at my next session with Jane. "I feel sadness for that little boy," I told her. "But I still struggle with my anger."

"What do you mean, 'struggle with your anger'?" Jane asked.

"I can feel how sad and alone I was as a child," I explained. "But I can't really get at my anger."

"You will," she said. "You will."

She was right. When it came, it was vicious.

I was drifting off to sleep one evening when Maddy, my five-year-old daughter, awoke from a nightmare. Groggy and still half asleep, I stumbled into her room and sat on the edge of her bed. Nightmares weren't real, I explained. They just seemed real. I turned on the light to show her that everything was okay and then, as she fell back to sleep, I sang her our favorite song, *You Are My Sunshine.* When her soft, slow breathing told me she was asleep, I started back to my room and, out of nowhere, it hit me.

What would I do if either of my daughters was in the same emotional pain I was in as a child? Would I respond differently than my parents had? Of course, I would! Would I be there for them? Of course, I would! To do anything else would be selfish. It would be bad parenting. With that realization, I got angry—very angry.

"I am *so fucking angry*!" I shouted.

Jane did not interrupt.

"You want to know the truth?" I said, bounding out of my chair, pacing angrily. "I'll tell you the *truth*! My parents were *not* there for me! Oh, sure, they had their *reasons*—their good intentions—their own bad upbringings. Frankly, I don't *care*! I endured *all* that childhood agony because of good intentions? Give me a fucking *break*!"

I couldn't calm down—didn't *want* to calm down. This purge was long overdue. "You were right!" I erupted with emotion. "Intentions mean *nothing* to a little boy! I can't let my mom and dad off the hook just because they weren't aware. That's the same reason I've let everybody off the hook all my life! Everyone has good intentions, right? I mean, parents are supposed to *be* there for their kids! That's their job! Good intentions? Talk about the ultimate "Get Out of Jail Free" card! I let *everyone* off the hook while I stuffed my anger and paid for everyone else's mistakes! I am *done* making excuses for them! *So what* if they had good reasons? Does my upbringing release me from my responsibility to my kids? No way! That's my job!"

I plopped myself into my chair. "Times were *different*? What a fucking pathetic excuse!" I raged. "They had tough parents? Well, so did I! And *I'm* there for my kids. They were just doing the best they could? So fucking *what*!"

Jane finally interrupted me. "How old do you feel right now, Steve?"

"Like ten years old," I said. "Maybe eleven. Yeah, like an angry, hurt ten year old." There I was, as a child, bursting with anxiety and pain from the natural losses of my youth and the invalidation of my anger—coupled with Catholic guilt and shame—and no one to turn to. It created a lot of repressed emotion.

Throughout my life and starting at a young age, I was taught to squelch any feelings of grief or sadness. As an adult, my feelings seemed jumbled and inappropriate—and they scared and confused me—so, rather than deal with something that seemed out of my control, I stuffed them, buried them, over and over again. When I was fired from my dream job, I must have been devastated, but I didn't feel it. Instead, I just carried on. When my brother Paul died at the age of 21, my feelings felt distant, not really part of myself. By the time my first marriage collapsed, I felt nothing—no anger, no sadness, nothing.

On the other hand, strong feelings sometimes flowed out of me, triggered by something superficial like the cheap sentimentality of an AT&T commercial. And, while I didn't get angry with my parents, slow drivers made me furious. Whenever such negative feelings leaked out, they seemed supernatural and out of control, as if they'd materialized out of thin air. And the more they seeped out, the more I tried to control them.

I could not (or would not) see the connection between these seemingly arbitrary feelings and repressed emotions, though I had all the symptoms. I drank every night. I was impulsive, to the point that it cost me my job and my marriage. My finances were a mess, though I earned good money. And, while I could feel something akin to happiness, I could not trust it to last. My self-deprecating humor and faux optimism convinced everyone that I was happy because I had all the trappings of "success": I made good money, had good kids, published a couple of books, and consulted to major corporations. The picture looked great.

As the fog cleared, another question arose that seemed odd at first. I noticed that I tried to exert control over my children and the women I was involved with. At first, I thought that I didn't do this any more than the next guy. I liked to give my opinion, I thought, but I certainly never told people what to do with their lives. Then it dawned on me: maybe I was an internal control freak? While I easily accepted that many things in life were out of my control, my *inner* life was another story.

"If I controlled my emotions that much," I asked Jane, "could I be a control freak?"

Sure, I thought, I could laugh, tell jokes and show consideration. But, when it came to sadness, anger or any of the "dark" emotions, I kept them under lock and key. I had been taught to exert incredible control over my feelings, so much so that I couldn't access my emotions when I needed them, when certain situations demanded some sort of emotional response. I was cut off. Though I was intellectually capable of *thinking* anger and sadness, I was unable to *feel* them.

When the emotional dam broke, I realized that much of my exhaustion came from working so hard to control my feelings. To accept that holding my feelings down gave me only an *illusion* of control—while my feelings were really backing up in my psyche—I had to bottom out and lose control, open the floodgates. I had to let go.

Since I had put off letting my emotions naturally surface, I had also put off processing and dealing with them. This included the feelings from ten years of my life.

Probing very soft tissue, Jane took it slowly. I was still often overwhelmed with acute and raw emotions, though I used my medication to help ease my intense anxiety.

All of my uncontrollable, pent-up feelings scared the hell out of me and I wanted to back away from the process.

"I don't know if I can do this." I told Jane soon after my anger surfaced.

"Do what?" she asked.

"Process these emotions," I said. "I can't seem to stop them. I mean, before, I had them under control and..."

She stopped me. "You *thought* you had them under control," she pointed out.

"Yeah," I said. "I mean, before, I was able to stuff them but, now, they well up and I find myself crying, sometimes uncontrollably."

"That's grief," said Jane. "You can't control grief. It works best if you just let it wash over you. You have to learn to let go of it, and that will help you get through it faster."

"How long does it take to process grief?"

Jane looked me in the eye. "How much grief do you have inside?" she asked. "Just let go and stay with the feelings."

"Just let go?" I asked. "Just let go? Do you *know* how hard that is? I've had them under control all my life and now I'm supposed to let them go? I cried last night for hours. My sides are sore from crying. I just want to take my meds and forget..."

" Steve, stay with the feelings," she said. "Don't stuff them again. You're doing great work."

"Great work?" I cried. "Come on! Is it normal for a 45 year old to cry for *days*? To want everyone who hurt me to feel the pain that I feel? Is it normal to want to break something—anything? I mean, a normal person wouldn't cry uncontrollably! A *normal* person wouldn't be this angry. That would be crazy, right?"

For the first time, Jane sounded angry. "You're wrong, Steve," she said. "*Not* crying was abnormal. Stuffing your anger and your sadness for so long was *abnormal*. We are *feeling* beings, and to deny your feelings is deny yourself. *Do not* back away from them."

Her confidence gave me strength to let go again as the emotion flooded in. My anger turned venomous while my sadness squeezed my heart and as the long-denied emotions rose to the surface of my psyche, I no longer wanted to stop them. They spilled over.

"You're right," I said. "I could have cried for a month about my brother's death alone and still have some left over!"

"*At least* a month." Jane said.

"All my life, I put up with people who invalidated my anger and grief," I said, clenching and unclenching my hands. "I *hate* them for that! *Fuck* them!" I couldn't sit still. Anger tensed my hands, my chest and my legs while the muscles in every part of my body tightened with a twelve-year-old boy's anger. I had to walk. I got up and began pacing like an angry animal. "*No one* has the right to invalidate my sadness!" I cried. "*No one* has the right to tell me I can't be angry. To *hell* with anyone who tries to tell me differently!"

I realized that it was no wonder I had spent so many years in therapy, avoiding real work. As this new process moved slowly forward, the feelings came in uncontrollable waves. On a rational level, I wanted to control them but, on an emotional level, I knew I had to let go in order to let my feelings exhaust their power over me.

Jane urged me to have faith in the process, to trust my instincts and feel the feelings. But, at times, surrendering to the process seemed impossible. For the longest time, I fought letting go, fearing that, if I let my emotions go, I would be crazy—not *go* crazy, but *be* crazy.

To make the journey more difficult, I found that the more I resisted the process and the emotions, the more anxious I became. Pandora's Box had blown open and I couldn't cram my feelings back inside. I was committed and there was no going back—and it was a *very* difficult swim.

To complete the journey, I had to accept that this would not be an intellectual process but an emotional journey. I struggled to get comfortable with that. Throughout my life, I had always used my *mind* to figure my way through challenges and I was good at "mastering" situations and problems intellectually. It was terrifying to realize that I couldn't *think* my way through this particular situation. Every time an emotion surfaced, I tried to find its origin so I could "solve" it and be done with it, but it didn't work that way. Dealing with emotions meant I had to muddle through a process that didn't follow sensible rules because the process of feeling feelings isn't linear, rational or logical.

That meant that I never knew the next step, which also meant that the process was riddled with ambiguity—*maddening* ambiguity.

"This is the process, isn't it?" I asked Jane a session or two after my explosion.

She knew what I was talking about. "Yes, it is," she said quietly.

"I didn't expect this much pain," I said. "It's agony, pure agony. *No wonder* I put it off. Before we started, I thought that *understanding* the process was the process."

"What do you mean?"

"I thought reading psychology and self-help books was the process," I explained. "I thought I'd learn how to use techniques to cope with my feelings. I thought deep *analysis* was the same as deep emotional work."

"And now?"

"The real process is feeling the feelings I stuffed for so long, feeling the anger and grief," I sighed. "The real process is crying so hard my sides ache and being knocked to the floor by my childhood grief. The real process is pulling off to the shoulder of the highway because I can no longer see through my tears."

"And getting your anger out in ways that don't hurt others or yourself," she added.

"I'm glad I didn't know how hard this was going to be," I admitted. "This is the hardest work I've ever done."

"The older you are, the tougher and longer the process," Jane said. "And I guess you think seeing me is the process as well?"

"Of course, it is," I stammered. "Isn't it?"

"Not really," she said. "We spend most of our time talking about the thoughts and feelings you've had over the past week. Sometimes when we meet, you get insights but mostly you walk in the door with them. You're doing most of the work on your own."

For months, my feelings bounced back and forth between rage and grief as I experienced wave after wave of gut-wrenching sadness, sometimes mixed with anger, sometimes alone. Ever so slowly, my overstuffed psyche emptied itself, dissipating the emotions. Rage turned into anger. Grief turned to sadness.

I just wanted it to end. Eager to get through the painful feelings as fast as possible, I tried to *manage* my sadness. Eventually, I learned the rules of grieving: It would be over when it was over; it would go as deep as it has to go; I was not in control. It was an incredibly difficult and necessary exercise in letting go.

The grieving process always started and ended the same way, beginning with anxiety and slowly sliding into exhaustion and confusion. If I distracted myself with alcohol, a relationship or some other avoidance behavior, I could continue to stuff my feelings. But, if I waited long enough and stayed with the feelings, they intensified, my grief and sadness surfaced, and the process began. Sometimes, I could pinpoint the trigger—usually a memory of a childhood experience—but, most times, I couldn't identify the source of a feeling. It just seemed to arrive, wipe me out, and then disappear like an emotional flu.

But, in the end, it didn't matter. Grief was grief, and when I went through it I always felt cleaner, like breathing fresh air after a good rain.

Jane reminded me that the intensity of my feelings had roots in my childhood and that the depth of my anger and grief was not appropriate to the situation *in the present.* This was a great piece of advice. Though I was angry with my parents for not giving me the love and support I needed *as a child*, it wasn't right for me, *as an adult,* to punish them now. My emotions were *childhood* emotions, not adult emotions.

I found other ways to release my pent up energy. Jane helped me ritualize the process. Though it sounds childish, I burned photographs and smashed mementos, which helped me to work out my anger. I found chopping wood to be therapeutic and I had the blisters to prove it. And slowly, ever so slowly, I learned to *feel* anger and grief instead of *thinking* these emotions.

At times, my anger also had a beneficial side: I used it to set boundaries. Normally easygoing and complacent about things—especially with my family—I learned to use my anger at my family to help me set boundaries with them, sometimes with a hammer. Eventually, my anger eased up.

In time, I also became good at identifying the physical signals that indicated I was falling back into my old patterns and stuffing my emotions. Jane said that I was very somatic (feeling emotional disturbances through physical manifestations) and I used this information provided by night sweats, aching muscles, stomach cramps, and diarrhea to come to understand my psyche's signals that I was avoiding or resisting some emotional work.

At times, I would start to notice that my anxiety ratcheted up with intrusive thoughts and inappropriate concerns. Within a few days, I would begin to feel exhausted, even after eight hours of sleep. Naturally, I would try to pinpoint the reasons for my anxiety and exhaustion, convincing myself that I must have caught a cold or flu. Eventually, though, it would dawn on me that the exhaustion, anxiety and intrusive thoughts came from trying to control the process—from resisting my feelings. Then, the dam would break as the feelings surged. With no control or suppression, I let the pure and intense feelings wash over me.

Jane noticed the changes before I did.

"Am I making progress?" I asked her one session. "I feel better but I can't really see my progress."

She laughed. "You wouldn't notice this but you haven't moved from your position on that couch for the entire session. You couldn't have done that a month ago."

"Really? You noticed that?"

"When you first came to see me, you couldn't sit still," she said. "You always played with your fingers or scratched at yourself, but I don't see any of those behaviors now."

She was right. I was starting to relax. A friend pointed it out as well. "You've stopped twitching," he told me. "You seem less nervous, less fidgety, and you're more relaxed. Not so hyper." He was right. I *was* able to sit still without playing with my hands or head.

As my emotional work began to pay off, other changes became clear. My mood started to brighten. My nails grew back. I stopped picking at my head. And the anxiety that had always plagued me claimed less of a hold such that, at times, I forgot about it completely. I underwent bigger changes, too.

"How's your drinking going?" Jane asked me.

"Pretty good," I said. "Remember, I used to have a beer every afternoon around 5 o'clock? And I cut it out when I began therapy with you?"

"Yes," she said, "I remember."

"Well, even though I stopped having my afternoon beer, I still wanted one in the afternoon," I explained. "But, the other day, I realized that my desire has vanished. And it's not just my desire for beer, but my desire for alcohol in any form."

"It isn't really about the alcohol," she said.

"It's not?"

"The real reason you feel less need for alcohol is because your anxiety has dropped so low that you no longer need to self-medicate."

"I didn't realize how much I used alcohol to handle my anxiety," I said. "I just thought I liked beer a lot."

"I'm sure it seemed that way," Jane said. "We have so many defense mechanisms that it's pretty hard to see your unhealthy behaviors when you're *in* them."

At times, the only evidence that I was making progress came after I had completed a particular stage of grief. A few weeks after an intense bout of grief, I began to notice subtle but profound changes. "Something's happening," I told Jane. "Something I didn't expect."

"What's that?" she asked me.

"Remember, I told you about my brother Paul?"

"The one who died of cancer?"

"Yes," I said. "Well, I never really grieved his death until we began this process but he feels different to me now."

"Different how?"

"I don't know if I can explain it," I said.

"Try."

"Before I grieved Paul's death, I always felt like I was carrying him on my shoulders, like a weight," I explained.

"And now?"

"It's like I feel him not *on* me but *in* me," I said. "My load is lighter. Since I got in touch with my sadness over his death, I'm able to let go of it. Not that I'll ever forget him..."

"It sounds as though you are integrating the loss into your life, coming to terms with it," Jane said.

"Yeah," I said. "I feel like I'm letting go of the emotional weight I carried and integrating his loss into who I am. Like I said, it is hard to explain."

"Does it feel okay?" Jane asked.

"That's the other thing," I said. "Even though I feel as though I'm letting go of Paul, accepting the loss, I feel somehow more complete, more whole. Does that make sense?"

"Yes," Jane nodded. "But a better word might be 'intact'."

"That's it!" I nodded. "More *intact*! It's weird that I let go of something yet I feel more *complete*."

"It has to do with boundaries." Jane said. "When you're secure with your boundaries, you feel more complete."

"What does *that* mean?" I asked.

"We'll get to that," she said.

I began to feel so good that I started to *look* for things to grieve about! I thought if I could just grieve some more, the changes would come even faster. I started to listen to sad songs, dug out childhood pictures, and tried to think of things that made me emotional. But the feelings wouldn't come. Still a control freak, I began to get discouraged with the process because I couldn't *make* the sadness and anger surface.

Days later, my faith was restored when grief unexpectedly welled up and I burst into tears. Though I never figured out why, it didn't really matter; it mattered only that *the process* was in charge. I wasn't.

During my years of searching up to that point, I had confused *knowing* the work with *doing* the work. That's why I got stuck, because I wasn't able to let go at the natural break-points in my life. Instead, I clung to my idealization of my parents, to my youth, to my expectations of life. Even at 45 years of age, as something of a 45 year-old teenager, I still believed that life should be more romantic than it really was, so I held on to an ideal from my childhood.

One time, when I was in college, I went to Rocket's house to pick him up for a soc-cer game. Noticing the unforced affection between him and his parents, I could tell that he genuinely liked them, and I found this realization both strange and discomforting. I couldn't pinpoint anything remarkable as his Mom hugged him when we started to leave and his Dad wished him luck from his recliner, but something was different in their relationship. Rocket was comfortable around his parents; I was always on guard with mine. Maybe experiencing unconditional love and support at critical stages of his life gave Rocket an internal security and foundation of self-esteem that I lacked.

As Rocket grew up, I watched him let go of the expectations of his youth. Always more mature than I was, he never seemed bothered that he was balding prematurely. He also seemed to feel that he could turn to his parents for support—any time. Providing the foundation upon which he could grieve his losses and move on, their support seemed to make him strong.

Once, on our annual summer vacation, I had an argument about unconditional love and support with my mom. We were sitting at the table after the dinner dishes were cleared when my mom raised the subject of how my sister had raised her kids. Mom was upset that my sister's oldest child still lived at home soon after graduating from college.

"That kid needs a swift kick in the pants," she said. "I wouldn't let *my* kids do that!"

"He's broke, but he's trying to get on his feet," I countered. "He'll move out when he finds a job."

"She pampers him," my mom argued, frowning. "We didn't do that to our kids. Once you finished college it was out the door—sink or swim."

"I think she's just giving him the support he needs right now," I said. "After all, he's only 22. That's still young."

"Oh, and what is she going to do when he's 30?" she challenged. "I had three kids by the time *I* was 22. He'd better grow up!"

"I don't agree," I said. "I think she's doing the right thing."

"Well, don't come crying to me when your daughters are still living with you when they are 35 years old!"

On the other hand, Rocket's parent's seemed to work under a philosophy that was fundamentally different from my parents'. His Mom and Dad seemed to believe that their unconditional support made their son more self-reliant, while mine believed that kicking kids out by a certain age made them stronger.

I know many parents who take credit for their children's positive achievements but blame their kids' emotional problems on genetics. I know from experience that it is easier to blame genes and other uncontrollable factors than it is to look in the mirror. But, after my own journey, I am convinced that we owe much of our emotional health—as well as our emotional dysfunction—to our parents' emotional support of us when we were in our developmental stages in childhood. I am a firm believer in nurture, not nature.

A friend recently asked me, "How you would feel if your daughter ended up in an abusive relationship?"

It was a surprising question but I did not hesitate to answer. "I'd feel as though I let her down," I answered without a second thought. "I'd think that somehow I'd made a mistake raising her."

This friend thought my answer was arrogant, that it was a sign of conceit and selfishness to think that I had so much influence on my daughter's choices. But I firmly believe my answer was both realistic and responsible. I am very willing to take responsibility for my successes and failures as a parent. And, because of this belief, I put a good deal of thought and care into how I raise my children. It has paid off for them.

As my therapy progressed, I began to feel much better. My anxiety was subsiding and my depression was gone. I decided to cut back on my weekly appointments with Jane.

Then I saw something that made me realize that I had a *lot* more work to do.

The Fifth Truth

As you do your work, the true sources of your anxiety and depression will reveal themselves.

"Beware the tired man for he is very angry."

—Beth Flynn

Jane began the session with a direct question. "Would you say that you and your father were close when you were young?" she asked.

That was interesting.

"No," I said. "He wasn't easy to get close to. Never was."

"Did he show much affection?" she probed. "Did you spend much time with him?"

"No," I said. "You know, he worked two jobs and had ten kids, so I didn't see him much."

"When you *did* have the opportunity to be with him," she pressed, "did you feel close to him?"

"I missed my dad," I said, "even when he was around."

Jane held me in a steady gaze so I continued.

"My dad defines himself as an intellectual," I began again. "He thrives on detail and the intellectual pursuit of knowledge. He's a historian, written something like 13 books. He's not an emotional guy."

Thinking about it, I realized that, when my Dad "hugs" me, he grasps my arm near my elbow and leans into me. Gawky and stiff, like someone trying to master an unfamiliar skill, he seems to have forgotten how to embrace another person. I know my Dad loves me very much, but he doesn't know how to show it. When his closest childhood friend died after a long bout with cancer, I wanted to give him a chance to talk about his friend, so I brought up his loss but I got nowhere. Even after such a devastating loss, he couldn't—or wouldn't—open up. Sad to see him so cut off from himself, I realized that he pays for it, and so do all of us McCourts—psychologically and physiologically.

"Surely you've seen your Dad show some emotion in your life?" Jane asked.

"Nope," I said. "Not unless jokes or sarcasm count as emotions. Most McCourts can tell a good joke but sadness or grief? Never."

"Even when your brother died?" she asked. "Didn't he cry then?"

"I never saw him lose it," I recalled. "Even at the funeral, he hid it from us."

"I'm sure he shared his feelings with your mom."

"No," I argued. "He didn't."

"How would you know?"

"I am sure of it," I said flatly. "She told me."

"Your mom told you that your dad didn't cry?" Jane asked. "I find that hard to believe."

"Well, not exactly," I said. "After Paul died, Mom told me that she wanted to talk about him but Dad wouldn't because it made him uncomfortable. Even today, if we talk about Paul, Dad stays out of the conversation."

"Hmm."

"He's always had trouble sharing his feelings," I explained. "He stuffed them! Why would he be any different than me?"

"How do you know?"

"He's got the McCourt Curse," I said. "The nervous behaviors, picking and scratching. He can't sit still." Wanting to believe that our anxiety was hardwired, I used to blame it on my McCourt genes. But I started to see that it wasn't so much *nature*, as *nurture*.

"Do you think your father *knows* he is anxious?" Jane asked.

"No one in my family thinks they're anxious," I said. "Even the ones on medication. I remember the session when you suggested I might be anxious."

"You got defensive."

"Right," I nodded. "Because I couldn't hide it from you. I thought my anxiety was self-contained, that no one else could see it. People always described me as high energy but, maybe, they meant anxious or hyper."

"Maybe," she said. "Tell me this, Steve. Does your father drink, too?"

"Same dose, same times as I used to," I said. "A beer before dinner, wine with dinner, beer after dinner. Like father, like son."

"Do you think he's an alcoholic?"

"If he is, then I am."

"Has your craving for alcohol returned?" she asked.

"Nope," I said. "I'd still rather not have it in my system, other than a glass of wine at night with my book. I don't really want any more than that."

"Sounds like your dad self-medicates."

"Every one in my family medicates!" I said. "We need something to help dampen down the emotions. We *all* use something to manage our anxiety. I used alcohol and relationships. Some of my siblings use medication. Some use alcohol. It's hard to admit it to ourselves..."

"What do you mean, you used relationships to medicate?"

"If I had someone else around, then I wouldn't have to deal with myself," I said. "I focused on her."

"So, is everyone in your family anxious?"

"Yes," I said. "But no one *looks* anxious." I realized that, as children, we all learned to stuff our anger, sadness, and affections and that, even today, we all struggle to control our feelings. Some of my siblings show almost no emotion, while others show too much as their feelings explode in nervous bursts. Some of us manage better than others do.

Acknowledging our family—not our genes—as the source of my problem was a big step that me to take responsibility for my problems. To take responsibility, I had to face the system in which I grew up.

"Men of your father's generation didn't show feelings easily," Jane continued.

"You know, it's funny," I said, "but I always imagined fathers as affectionate, caring and present, even though my dad wasn't like that. He was formal, aloof. Actually, that's how most dads were. I never saw any of my friends' fathers show affection."

"Even Rocket's?"

"Yeah," I said. "He was the same. I never saw him show emotion."

"Really?" Jane asked. "Was he more affectionate than your dad?"

"Maybe a little," I said. "But not much. But, then, I don't know if Rod's dad shared his feelings with his wife, and I *know* my dad didn't share much with my mom. Is that usual?"

"I think it was the norm," said Jane. "But that doesn't make it healthy."

"Thinking about it, I think that the closest my Dad came to showing me affection was tickling me until I almost puked," I offered.

"Does he have an easier time showing affection now?" she asked. "Or does it seem more difficult for him?"

"He tries," I said. "He really tries and I love him for it, but he has a tough time. He just doesn't know how, or he forgot how. "

"Has he ever told you how much he loves you?" Jane asked me.

"Nope," I answered. "Never. It's as if he can't bring himself to say it. I tell my kids all the time, but I think that men of my dad's era believed showing emotion was a sign of weakness. Seems like a generational thing."

"But that's not true of *all* emotions." Jane pointed out.

"What do you mean?"

"What about anger?" Jane asked. "Did you ever see your father get angry?"

"Not really," I said. "No, wait. Yes, he got angry with us kids but never at anyone else."

"Ever see him get angry with your mother?"

"Never," I said. "Not even frustrated with her." I paused. "That seems weird, doesn't it?"

"Did he ever hit you?" she asked. Her question hung in the air for a minute.

"Yes," I finally admitted. "He hit us a lot."

A whole family ritual had grown up around punishment with The Belt. According to family lore, Dad took the belt off a dead Japanese soldier in World War II but, when I was an adult, I learned that that Dad had never seen combat. Since Dad was part of the occupation forces helping to rebuild Japan after the surrender, if he took the belt off of a dead soldier, it wasn't someone he had killed.

Once, I set the field behind our house on fire. An abandoned golf course, it was overgrown with weeds and hay and, a couple of times a year, someone would light a match to it. Once, at my sister's encouragement, I was the arsonist. Then, she turned me in to my mom who sent me to my room to await Dad—and The Belt.

That was the ritual. First, you endured the psychological torture of waiting in your room until Dad arrived. Once he came in, you pulled down your pants and knelt next to the bed. Dad rolled up his sleeves and applied the number of swats he deemed appropriate to the crime. Very abusive, it was also very common in the 1960s. After he finished, he left you alone to think about what you did to deserve his wrath.

"Were you the only one he hit with the belt?" Jane asked.

"No, I said. "My older siblings and I all got the belt. But, come to think of it, I don't remember any of the younger kids getting it."

"Is that the only way he'd ever hit you?"

"Well, in addition to the belt, he'd slap me with his hand."

"Open hand or fist?"

"Open hand," I said, as if it let him off the hook. "Never with his fist."

"How did you feel when he hit you?" Jane asked me.

"Well, I never wanted to give him the satisfaction of seeing me cry," I said. "So I always fought back my tears. And I remember being scared."

"Of what?"

"Not of being hit, really," I said. "Something else. I can't put my finger on it."

Jane waited.

My awareness came slowly. "It's like my dad wasn't really angry until *after* he started hitting me."

"What do you mean?"

"Well, Dad has a sort of poker face but, once he started with the belt, he was like out of control."

Jane sat forward. "Go on," she said.

"Other than this, I've never seen my dad act out of control," I explained. "I mean, even when he eats, he demonstrates a great deal of self-control."

"What do you mean by 'self-control'?"

"He eats his meals as if he's conducting a symphony," I explained. "He orchestrates every bite with the precise amount of each food on his plate, and finishes with the same proportions of each item. His last bite always contains the same amount of each item. And he never has anything left over."

Jane laughed. "I don't know which is stranger," she said. "Your dad's eating habits or the way you obsess about it!"

"Yeah," I smiled. "My Dad's a control freak—just like I am!"

"And your point is?"

"My point is that the only time in my life that I ever saw my dad lose control was when he hit me or my siblings," I said. "I've seen him knock my sisters to the floor with his hand."

"Oh, no!" Jane said, looking truly astonished. "How terrible to experience that and to witness it as a child. But tell me what you mean by him losing control."

"Well, I felt like he couldn't stop," I said. "One time, he started in and something flashed across his face and then he had a tough time stopping. It was scary."

"Scary?"

I was very afraid of my dad's anger. Once, when I was 16 years old, I was showing off to a girl by hanging from a train trestle near our house. I looked up to see my dad standing above me. He just said, 'Get Home!' and I knew I was in for it. I might have been better off letting go. He hit my hip so hard that The Belt left black and blue marks bigger than my hand. My Mom saw the marks but refused to believe that my father was responsible.

"That must have been scary for both of you," Jane said.

"Yeah, but it was more terrifying to see him so out of control," I said. "It seemed like he was wrestling with his anger. Like if he really let go he might not be able to stop."

"So when you saw anger…"

"It was always out of control," I interrupted.

"That's a strong reason to fear your emotions," Jane suggested.

Jane had made a connection that I'd never realized. I knew that, as a kid, my anger and sadness were never acceptable and my feelings were never justified. On top of that, when I was young and saw my Dad lose control of his feelings, I learned that emotions *needed* to be controlled. The connection made sense on an intuitive level. It wasn't something I could think through. And there was more, as my awareness gathered momentum.

"Did you ever see your father in a situation where he was vulnerable?" Jane asked.

"Vulnerable?" I asked. "I mean, I understand the word 'vulnerable' but I don't think I know what you mean by it."

"Well, did you ever see your dad ask for help from anyone?" she asked. "Like your mother, a friend, or his family?"

I laughed. "My Dad has the worst golf swing in the world," I said. "But he won't even take a lesson to try and correct it. No, I've *never* seen him ask for help, from *anyone.*"

"Do you think he's uncomfortable asking for help?" Jane asked.

"Yeah, he feels threatened having to lean on someone else," I said. "Like when I connected his computer to the Internet, he didn't know how to use it but, for a really long time, he wouldn't ask me or anyone else for help. He had to learn it himself because asking for help might make him look weak."

"How do you know that?" Jane asked. "You sound very sure and I'm having a problem with that."

"Well, he's like me," I said. "I have a problem asking for help—or I used to, anyway. The McCourt men have a problem being vulnerable."

"Okay, so how about your brothers?" Jane pried. "Are you close to them?"

"No," I said. "None of us are what I would call close. I mean, we get together for holidays, play golf and stuff, but close? Not really. We don't share intimate feelings or thoughts."

"Do you think your brothers struggle with their feelings like you did?"

"I *know* they do."

"Do they have problems expressing their feelings?" she asked. "Have you ever seen your brothers cry, for example?"

"No," I said. "The day after my wife and I broke up, I was with my brother and I was really upset. He didn't know what to do and I could tell that it made him *very* uncomfortable. All he could say was, 'What are you going to do now? You're going to be a single dad again so you're going to have to find a steady job. You won't be able to be a consultant anymore.' "

"Hmmm," Jane murmured, encouraging me to continue.

"He didn't know what to say," I said. "I know that he was trying to be there for me but he made me feel worse, not better."

"Sounds pretty cut off to me."

"Yeah," I said vaguely. "He meant well, but he didn't have a clue what I really needed. And I'm sure that the intensity of my feelings scared him."

"Well, what did you want from him?" Jane asked. "If he could have done something to help you feel better, what would that have been?"

"Just put his arm around me, tell me it will be okay, and listen," I said, pausing. "That's what I needed. That's all I wanted from Dad when I fell down and hurt myself."

"Right," Jane said softly. "That's all we want—someone to be there for us physically and emotionally."

I began to see patterns I had never noticed before. Not just Dad and my brothers but my brothers-in-law as well, all the men in my family struggle with their feelings. In fact, I realized, almost every male I knew had the same problem. I wanted to ask my sisters if they had the same problem with their husbands and if they struggled with the same intimacy issues. Did they complain about their husbands the way my wives did about me? Did they think their husbands didn't need them?

"My Dad keeps his emotions under such tight control, I don't think anyone knows him in a way that he finds satisfying," I told Jane. "He's cut off from his feelings. Maybe even more than I was."

"Like a lot of men of his generation," Jane said.

"Yeah, he never seemed to need anyone, not even my Mom," I said. "He always seemed self-assured and confident, but I think he thought that suppressing his emotions would help me become a man. In fact, I *am* a lot like that—equating vulnerability with weakness."

"And?"

"I learned to control my emotions," I said. "But, in the process, I lost touch with them, cut myself off from my feelings."

"What do you mean, 'cut off'?"

"Like in my work," I said. "I work with a lot of executives and, in the corporate world, emotion can be a sign of weakness. Showing your feelings can cost you."

"Is that just the way it is in business?"

"Yeah, just the way it is," I nodded. "But, when you asked about my Dad sharing his feelings with my Mom, it got me thinking."

"You were pretty confident that he didn't."

"Right, but I've been thinking about the difference between *controlling* emotions and being *cut off* from them."

"Interesting distinction," Jane raised her eyebrows. "Go on."

"Well, I'm sure some executives are cut off from their feelings as well, but I've met healthy, happy managers, too," I said. "They don't seem repressed, yet they still keep their emotions under control in business situations. Maybe, when they step out of the spotlight, they open up with someone—their partner or spouse, someone they trust. When it's safe."

"The distinction being?"

"My point is that my Dad didn't just control his feelings," I said. "He *compartmentalized* them. I did the same thing, cut myself off from my feelings. That's why they seemed so alien at first." I paused.

"Oh, man!" I blurted.

"What is it?" Jane asked.

"I just thought of something!" I said. Thinking about my relationships, I realized that all of them began the same way, as I quickly shared deep, intimate feelings. But, later, all of those relationships also ended the same way, as I became silent, distant, and cut off. It's not that I made a *conscious* decision to cut myself off from the women in my life, but that they didn't get to know me. It was starting to come together. "Almost every woman I ever dated had the same complaint about me. They all said I seemed so independent that they felt like I didn't need them."

"Oh, really?"

"Maybe I'm more like my dad than I thought."

"In what way?"

My insight was emerging as I spoke. "You know how I've been working hard on my feelings…"

"Yes," Jane nodded.

"I controlled—stuffed—my feelings for so long that I'd lost touch with them, couldn't access them, just like my Dad…"

"Go on."

"And I thought, if I couldn't access them, how could anyone else access them?" I said. "Does that make sense?"

"Yes," Jane said. "But complete your thought."

"My girlfriends and wives all said I seemed too…" I was frustrated, searching for a word. "Too…"

"Invulnerable?" Jane offered.

"That's it, invulnerable! T hey felt that I didn't need them, that I was invulnerable," I said. "Because I didn't have access to my feelings, no one else had access to them either. Does that make sense?"

"Yes, but it's incomplete," Jane said. "Keep going."

"Incomplete?" I asked. "I can't figure out the connection between controlling my emotions and being invulnerable or vulnerable. Most of the women in my life complained that

I didn't share enough with them and felt like I didn't need them. But, damn. It just won't come. I can't see it."

"Try 'intimacy,'" Jane suggested.

"Intimacy?" I asked. "What's *this* got to do with intimacy? Well, actually, what *is* intimacy?"

"Part of intimacy is being vulnerable with another person, letting them see you as you truly are," Jane explained.

"And that would mean sharing my feelings!"

"You are doing great work, Steve," Jane said. "See how you need to *feel* the connection, rather than think it through?"

"By stuffing my emotions—controlling my emotions and cutting myself off from them—I didn't have *access* to them!" Something fell into place. "Got it!" I added. "I didn't have access to my emotions so no one else had access to them either. Cutting myself off means that I cut *everyone* off! So the more I controlled my feelings, the less capacity I had for intimacy."

"Stay with your feelings, Steve," Jane said. "Go on…"

"I could only let people know me as well as I knew myself," I said. "Control and intimacy canceled each other out! So, no wonder they saw me as invulnerable!"

"Great work," Jane said. "Do you realize that you couldn't have seen that a few weeks ago? You didn't have the distance."

"Yeah," I answered. "And I see the connection between my anxiety, controlling my emotions and the pattern of my relationships. Being in touch with their own feelings gives people the capacity for intimacy."

"There's more to intimacy than just being in touch with your feelings," said Jane.

"Like what?" I asked.

"We'll get to that," she said. "Be patient. Just stick with your feelings for now."

But I started thinking about friends of mine who dated "unavailable" people—married or attached people, workaholics who would never make time for a relationship, "geographically undesirable" people…They all complained about their partners and, all along, I had thought that I was above that, but here I was, just like the emotionally unavailable partners that my friends ended up with.

"I feeling something I never knew I could feel," I told Jane.

"Can you describe it?" Jane asked. "Is it anxiety?"

"No, anxiety is bad," I said. "This is a *good* feeling, but different. I don't know if I can explain it but I feel more whole."

"More self-possessed?" she suggested.

"That's it!" I said. "That's the word I was searching for! Self-possessed! I feel as if I own my life more." *Self-possessed*, I thought with a smile. The term made sense to me.

When I had started the work, I hadn't felt complete. I didn't feel that way until I was able to integrate my feelings into my whole being. Now, I was beginning to feel emotionally healthy as I experienced life in a more fulfilling, complete way. Life became more enjoyable—like a black and white film that's had its color restored.

My feelings seemed more appropriate to a given situation. I stopped crying at the manipulative, tearjerker AT&T commercials and felt true sadness for people dealing with difficulty in their lives. It was appropriate sadness and concern!

"How is your anxiety level?" Jane asked.

"Much lower," I reported. "I don't get as nervous as I used to, either, and it's actually kind of peaceful. Quiet. I didn't expect this."

She smiled.

"By the way," I added, "last week, something small but important happened."

"What was that?"

"I had to fly down to San Jose to work with clients," I said. "Now, in the past, I'd always become really anxious on take-off but, this time, it didn't bother me at all. In fact, as the flight took off, I became aware of how relaxed I was!"

"Steve, that's great work," she said. "Great work!"

I was beginning to see not just the patterns but the *source* of my problems. I never imagined how deep I might have to look to see the roots of my emotional issues but, since they were intertwined with *all* the factors in my life—my family, my relationships, my feelings, *and* my genes, I realized that it was impossible to get any real relief by dealing with them separately. I couldn't compartmentalize my therapy any more successfully than I had compartmentalized my feelings. I had to go the distance. I had to be willing to look at *everything*.

I felt much better as my anxiety level was low and I hadn't had a panic attack or bout of depression in over a year. But something still bothered me. I knew that there was one topic we hadn't covered:

What about *Mom?*

The Sixth Truth

If we don't do our work, we pass on our anxious and depressive patterns to our children.

═══════════════════════════════════════

"Our attitudes and actions toward people of the opposite sex are a reflection of our unconscious attitudes toward our parent of the opposite sex."

—Stephen Mitchell,
Translator of the Tao Te Ching

"Were you promiscuous?" Jane began.

"What do you mean?" I asked. "I'm a guy."

"Did you sleep around when you were younger?"

"When I got the chance," I said. "Don't most guys?"

"Maybe," Jane said. "But that doesn't mean it's healthy. Tell me a bit about your relationships. How did they usually start?"

"Most of them started the same way," I explained. "Meet someone, fall in love and get serious pretty quickly."

"What do you mean 'quickly'?"

"Well, like my first wife," I said. "We worked together at a restaurant for a couple of months, flirted with each other a lot. One night, we went out on a date and ended up back at her place, in bed together. I moved in the next day."

"Wow! That really is fast," Jane said. "Moving in after the first date!"

"Most of my relationships started that way," I said. "When I fell in love, it usually happened pretty quickly. I love the intimacy."

"What intimacy?"

"You know, sleeping together," I answered.

"You think that's intimacy?"

"Isn't it?"

"Physical intimacy is only one part of a much bigger picture," said Jane.

"Don't you think people can fall in love?"

"Yes, but I think our definitions of 'falling in love' are different," Jane said. "Let me ask you this: Did your feelings last? Or did you fall out of love?"

I didn't like where she was going. This was not a door I wanted to open, because my relationships didn't just start the same way, but they all ended the same way, too. Sooner or later, the honeymoon would be over. Then , we'd run out of subjects to talk about. Sex was no longer great, but would become routine and then, eventually, we'd end up living together in a celibate friendship. As my soul mate became my roommate, our life together became boring. That was the pattern I repeated over and over again.

Still, I persisted in believing that my next relationship would be with my one true love, as I never lost faith in the romantic ideal of a soul mate. Just as Disney movies promised romantic love, I took the bait—hook, line and sinker—and then, when the romance dried up, I felt cheated and confused.

"Don't you think people have to work at a relationship?" I asked Jane.

"Yes, I do," she said. "But there has to be a healthy basis to work with."

"What do you mean 'healthy'?"

"Intimate relationships are possible between two mature people," said Jane. "When people trust each other, intimacy grows."

"I trusted my first wife," I said. "The first time we slept together, I told her things I never shared with anyone."

"That's what bothers me," she said. "You can't develop that level of trust in one night. It takes *time* for trust to develop."

"So you're saying we weren't intimate? How can you say that?"

"I'm not saying you didn't have some level of intimacy," she said. "How long did that feeling between you last?"

"Well, all my relationships eventually ended up loveless," I admitted. "No matter how much I worked at it, things just got old. But a lot of my friends say the same thing about their relationships."

"And are they happy?"

"Some of them are," I said. "But they all have a lot of problems with their partners and most of them have given up on being happy."

"What kind of problems?"

"Most of them complain about sex," I said. "You know…it lacks stimulation…their partner doesn't understand them…the usual stuff."

"How do they deal with it?"

"Some cheat, some learn to live with it, some stay single," I said. "I know some friends who even started swinging to spice up their love lives."

"I don't see how adding other partners simplifies the situation," said Jane dryly.

"One friend told me she solved the intimacy problem in her marriage," I said. "She has a husband to pay the bills and help raise a family, but then she sleeps with other guys for emotional nourishment, for the adventure. She calls it a 'perfect relationship'."

"Cheating on her husband is a perfect relationship?"

"Yeah," I said. "That's how she gets both economic and emotional satisfaction."

"Sounds like a gross rationalization to me."

"Most of my friends think relationships are something you just endure," I said.

"They don't have to be a burden," replied Jane. "Tell me more about the women in your life. What were they like, these women you dated?"

"Most of them had issues," I said. "Some of them were older, some were younger, but they were always struggling emotionally. Some of them were financially independent but they still needed to be taken care of. It seemed like I attracted women who were emotionally needy."

"Okay," Jane said. "How was your relationship with your mom?"

"My *mom*?" I asked. "What the...What does Mom have to do with my wives?"

"Did you have a good relationship with your mom when you were growing up?" she asked.

"Yeah," I began. "We had a great relationship. For a long time, I was her favorite. She gave me special attention and always treated me differently from my other siblings, like she let me sit in the front seat of the car when we went to church. So they were very jealous. Even today, they all say I was Mom's favorite."

"You say she treated you differently?" Jane asked. "What do you mean by that?"

"We were very close."

"How close?"

"Well, if you think there was any kind of abuse, you're barking up the wrong tree," I said. "I know Mom never abused me. Never."

"I'm not suggesting that at all," Jane said. "But, tell me more about your special relationship with your mom."

"We were very close," I said. "In grade school, I walked home every day just to have lunch with her."

Jane stopped me, looking perplexed. "How far was the school from home?"

"About a mile."

"How long did you have for lunch?"

"An hour," I said. "Why? What does that have to do with anything?"

"I just wonder why a ten-year-old boy would walk two miles a day to be with his mother for half an hour."

"I don't understand what you're getting at," I said.

"That's a long way to go for lunch," she repeated.

"What are you suggesting?"

"Nothing," Jane said. "Just something you should look at."

I enjoyed a special relationship with my mom, so I didn't see any problem with having gone home for lunch each day. Many mornings after Mom dropped me at school, she would attend Mass in the chapel next to the school and, sometimes, I would pretend to be sick so my teacher would let me go over to the chapel and ask Mom to take me home. One time, my Mom grew furious with me and said she couldn't even attend Mass without me bothering her. I was devastated.

"You seem to remember that vividly," Jane observed.

"Well, yeah," I said as my eyes filled up. "I remember how tough it was to be rejected by my mom. I still feel a lot of grief about that. When I went to school, I missed her a lot."

"I think that's normal," Jane said. "All children experience separation anxiety at first, but most kids get over it quickly. I guess I wonder why you missed her so much that you would walk home every day."

"I was a very insecure child," I said, feeling sorry for myself again. "I must have felt very lonely. I mean, I pestered her so much she stopped going to morning Mass."

"A ten-year-old boy walking two miles each day to have lunch with his mother is *not* about the boy," Jane said. "Its about his mother."

"*What?*" I asked as my anger shot to the surface. "How could it be about my *mother?*" I felt angry at Jane for being unfair to my mother. "*I* was the one who wanted to go home, who wanted her to take me home from Mass everyday. It wasn't her. It was me. She didn't do anything wrong!"

"Okay, Steve," said Jane. "Okay."

"How could it have been her?" I went on. "I made the decision to walk home every day and to fake being sick every morning."

"I'm sorry," Jane said. "But can a ten-year-old boy *really* make that decision on his own?"

"Are you saying my mother *used* me?"

"I'm saying a ten-year-old child doesn't decide to walk two miles each day without being influenced."

Leaving Jane's office, my anxiety flooded back. My mouth dried up and my head hurt. *Just like old times*, I thought. Exhausted by the anxiety, I was wracked with dry heaves in the parking lot. I didn't understand it. I needed time to think.

I couldn't just accept Jane's premise. My mother would never use me to meet her own intimacy needs. That would be wrong and manipulative. She and I had a special relationship. But, then, why *did* I walk all that way when I had children to play with at school? None of my siblings went home for lunch, and none of my brothers had a "special" relationship with Mom, like I did.

Could Jane be right? I wondered if I had replicated my relationship with my mother with all the women in my life. Sometimes I took care of my partners financially, but I *always* took care of them emotionally and, even if a woman started out independent, she always ended up dependent on me. Eventually, I felt smothered by them.

Why couldn't she be on her own more? I would wonder. *Why does she need me so much? Why do I have to support her? Why did she drift away from her girlfriends and emotionally rely on me so much?* After talking to Jane, I wondered if I had created the dynamic. Maybe it was a self-fulfilling prophecy...

With overwhelming anxiety, I had a tough week and fell back on regular doses of Ativan. Discouraged by my lack of progress, I felt as if I'd done all this work and yet I was back to Square One—and losing ground fast.

"I've been having a tough time this past week," I started the next session.

"You want to talk about it?" Jane asked.

"Yeah," I said. "I think I'm angry at my mom. I feel like she used me."

"Used you?" Jane asked. "How?"

"I think she used me to take care of her," I said, "to meet her emotional needs."

"You mean when you went home for lunch?"

"Yeah," I said. "I can't think of any other reason why a little kid would walk all that way. There were other things too."

"Like what?"

"Like, I got to sit in the front seat all the time," I said. "No one else was allowed to do that."

"Oh?"

"Yeah," I said. "One summer, we drove all over Europe, in a station wagon, and guess who sat between Mom and Dad the entire time?"

"Let me guess," Jane smiled.

"I feel something like anger," I said. "But I can't really get at it."

"Take your time," she said. "If it's there, it'll surface."

"I can understand why she might do something like that," I said. "Since my dad is so cut off, maybe she felt lonely and wanted company."

"Does that mean she wasn't responsible?" Jane asked.

"Well, yes, she was responsible," I said. "But she had her reasons. I mean, I can understand her loneliness, even if she wasn't aware of it. So, yeah, she was responsible, but I don't want to get angry at her for it."

"You're thinking like a 46-year-old man again," Jane pointed out. "But you need to feel like a 12-year-old child. If you go back to your trip in Europe, does that little boy feel angry?"

"Yes," I answered. "Angry and hurt, *very* hurt. He can't believe someone he trusted so much could do something like that, even if she *did* have a good reason." Anger rose into my throat and I felt it strangling me.

"So," Jane said, "since Mom had good reasons for her behavior, you're going to let her off the hook? Another 'Get Out Of Jail Free' card, Steve?"

I fought tooth and nail to deny what I now knew happened, figuring that my mom must have had a good reason. *She was just doing what lots of mothers do, right?* Sympathetic with my mother's dilemma, I reasoned that she hadn't been aware of how she'd used me. Like so many men of his generation, my Dad kept his emotions in check to the extent that he was emotionally aloof, cut-off. Mom needed some emotional nurturing, some form of intimacy, but…from *me*?

Our next session was crucial and potentially very dangerous for Jane. "How are you feeling?" she asked me.

"Angry," I answered with a low growl. "*Very* angry. How could a mother do that to a child? How could she use me to get her needs met?" Having difficulty controlling the rage that came to the surface, I went on. "Sure, she must have felt lonely. She must have felt so little intimacy in her life that she needed me. I made her feel like someone cared for her—but how *damaging*!"

"It's important to get in touch with that anger," said Jane. "It's a turning point for you."

"If she was in a sterile relationship, then tough luck for her," I said. "She should have found *another* way to get her needs met, *not* through me, for Christ's sake! No wonder all my relationships have been fucked up! No *wonder* I've always ended up with women who need me to take care of them. I was *looking* for them!"

"You have a right to be angry," said Jane. "I don't want to invalidate that, but do you understand your mom's reasons for creating that relationship?"

"Sure," I said. "Even if she was aware of it, she couldn't have discussed it with my dad. But she's *still* responsible for it and that makes me furious!"

"Stay with the feelings, Steve," Jane guided me.

"I don't want to be angry at Mom," I said. "She was doing the best she could but, still, she had no right!" My muscles tightened and my fists clenched as I felt like I was choking, torn between empathy and rage. "How could anyone *do* that to a child?" I steamed. "I trusted her and she *used* me! I don't care about her reasons; I don't care how *her* father or *my* father treated her. I just don't care! I can't *afford* to care. I need to get this *out!*"

"You're not alone," Jane said in a soft voice, almost a whisper. "Many parents get their intimacy needs met through their kids. It is kind of an epidemic."

"No parent has the right to use a child to make them feel better," I said, feeling broken. "It's just so *wrong*, so selfish! No wonder it's so hard to grow up, with our parents working against us. Just because they aren't aware of it doesn't mean they aren't responsible!"

I didn't want to believe it, but the proof in my relationships was blindingly obvious. I always—always, *always*—found a woman whom I could take care of, unconsciously seeking out women who needed me in some way. It was part of my psyche, part of *me*. I was naturally uncomfortable with secure, independent, mature women who didn't need me. I never dated one because I wasn't aware of them, didn't even know what such women looked like. They weren't on my radar and I wasn't on theirs.

A therapist once pointed out to me that I always became involved with women who had problems. Calling them wounded birds, he advised me to find someone who was healthier. That therapist wasn't wrong; he just didn't go far enough. *Intellectual* understanding of my pattern couldn't change my choices because I hadn't done the tough emotional work to heal those specific wounds. That work was absolutely necessary.

Now, my rage was bottomless. My mom couldn't handle her own feelings and, in her denial, she had so much damage, caused so much anguish for so many years. *God Dammit!* I thought, furious as I cried tears of profound sadness. Exhausted, I couldn't sit still. Instead, I paced my living room as I struggled to absorb my emotions without letting them overwhelm me.

It took me weeks to get through this final struggle but, as my emotions wrung themselves dry and as my psyche slowly emptied, I felt no anxiety, only a growing peace and clarity. Finally, I could see and touch the source of my problems.

"Alexis is ten years old, isn't that right?" Jane said.

"No, she's eleven," I corrected her.

"Would she walk two miles a day to spend half an hour with you?" she asked.

"Well, no," I said. "But we don't have the same relationship as I had with my mom. I'm her father and..." I stopped and then blurted, "Holy shit!"

"What is it?" Jane asked.

"I just remembered something in-fucking-credible," I said.

"Yes?"

"A while ago, my dad told me that he flunked fifth grade," I said. "It surprised me that someone as smart as my dad would fail anything, but he said the reason he flunked was because he missed too many days, sick."

"Yes?"

"Then he admitted he hadn't really been sick," I said. "But that his mom kept him home because she missed him. She signed the excuse notes for him every day. Hmmm."

Jane waited, knowing what was to come.

"Oh, God!" I said. "I see it!"

"It's right in front of you," Jane said.

"It is so simple," I said. "So simple. The pattern—the pattern...We pass it on!"

"Of course we do," Jane said, matter-of-factly.

"I went home each day because my mother needed me to come home," I said. "And my grandmother kept my dad home from the fifth grade because *she* needed *him.*"

The curtain flew open, revealing the whole structure of the mother-son relationships in the McCourt family. How could I *not* have seen it? My grandmother met her needs through my dad, his mother got her needs met through him, my mother got her needs met through me, and I...

Oh, my God. Oh, my God! Could I be using *my* children to meet my own intimacy needs? Was I passing along the dynamic to my daughters?

But, then, it wasn't just a McCourt thing anymore. The pattern was so obvious. I couldn't *not* see it! In churches, schools, and at kids' soccer games—indeed, across our society—I saw the pattern everywhere; fathers more intimate with their daughters than with their wives and mothers using their sons instead of their husbands for emotional nourishment.

Then, all my earlier pursuits of psychology came flooding back: Campbell, Jung, Freud, Rich. I recognized it as a universal archetype, which all cultures face, and which all cultures address differently.

My neighbor, who is working on her Ph.D. in psychology, told me of a coming-of-age ritual used in an African tribe. In the days before the ritual, the mothers pamper their sons, doing everything for them, doting on them, and taking them into their beds to sleep. Basically, the mothers treat their sons like infants. Then, as the ritual begins, the men of the tribe "kidnap" the boys from their mothers and take them into the bush. Then, each boy must hunt and kill a wild animal and live on his own for a period. Like many transitions to manhood, pain is part of the ritual, so the boys are circumcised. At the end of their time alone in the bush, the young boys gather on one side of a stream, while their mothers gather on the opposite bank. Then, the boys shout, scream, curse and rant at their mothers on the other side. While the entire village supports and protects the mothers on the shore, the boys across the river scream whatever they want at their mothers, for that time only. In this particular tribal culture, this ceremony is not only considered acceptable, but a critical part of the maturing process. I was fascinated by this part of the ritual, which resonated with me.

Joseph Campbell writes about similar separation rituals in other cultures, where the son is torn away from his mother as a necessary passage to manhood. Similarly, my process with Jane was also an individuation ritual.

Once I accepted the dynamic, my anger poured out in torrents. Terrifying, it tore my heart out, because what came from me was not mature emotion, but the rage of a ten-year-old boy magnified through the lens of 36 years. I ranted, I cursed, and I smashed things.

"I've been thinking a lot about the kind of women I'm attracted to," I told Jane.

"Really?" she asked. "Do you have a type that you end up with?"

"Yeah," I said. "They always had problems."

"What kind of problems?"

"Well, I never felt comfortable with independent women," I said. "Assertive, mature women have always intimidated me. And most of the women I've ended up with had serious issues with their fathers."

"What kinds of issues?"

"Everything from dads that weren't around to outright sexual abuse," I explained.

"Sounds like a pattern," Jane nodded. "Can you see why you were more comfortable with them?"

"I could make them feel better, save them from their problems," I said. "My dad always joked with my mother that, if it weren't for him, she'd still be living in poverty with her sisters in South Philly."

"Do your aunts live in poverty?"

"No," I said. "Dad just likes to tease her by saying that, like raising ten kids on a professor's salary was a piece of cake. Anyway, the acorn doesn't fall far…" I smiled.

Someone once told me that promiscuous people are the ones most terrified of intimacy. That had never made sense to me, because I had always pictured myself as a sensitive and caring lover. How could *I* be incapable of intimacy?

Most of my women friends have complained that the men they meet are immature and afraid of commitment. I realize that, perhaps, mine was not such an isolated case; maybe we all replicate the relationships we learned as children.

But, then, it would have to be the same for women. All of the women with whom I've had relationships had serious issues with their fathers, from fairly harmless emotional invulnerability to damaging sexual abuse. Their fathers all had boundary issues, and were either inaccessible or too lax in their boundaries. Most of these women never broke free of their childhood relationship and then they ended up with me—someone, just like their fathers, who would take care of them.

I always met women who were perfect for me, who were as emotionally immature as I was. So it wasn't just me. It was *us*. Searching for a relationship I couldn't handle, I sought intimacy of which I was incapable. In such a fruitless, ironic search, I slept with women and called it intimacy. In this way, my promiscuity made a kind of bizarre sense.

I saw the pattern: It fit. Men went to bars to pick up women who went to bars to meet men who went to bars to pick up women. It all made sense.

Do men prove their masculinity by overcoming women's reluctance to go home with them? Do self-respecting women go to bars to reject men who try to pick them up? If so, what the hell were we all *doing*? The women I met wanted to find someone who could make a commitment but, instead, they went home with me, hoping to turn a one-night stand into a long-term relationship. On a rational level, none of this made sense because it wasn't an intellectual pattern but an *emotional* one.

Women who need to be taken care of find men who need to take care of women. Men who are emotionally invulnerable find women who lack the capacity for intimacy. The most promiscuous people are those most afraid of intimacy. Our relationships are our mirrors. We form relationships with friends and lovers based on the amount of intimacy that we are capable of nurturing. No one is any more damaged or healthy than ourselves.

My brother was right. After my second divorce, he told me that I would quickly find another woman. "You won't stay single for long," he said smugly. "That's not your pattern. And I know the type of woman you'll end up with."

His cocksureness pissed me off, but I bit. "What do you mean?"

"You always end up with the same type of woman—young, pretty and slim." he said. "That's your type."

The bastard nailed it! I would end up with a woman who was exactly the same as all the others. Even if the next woman wasn't young, pretty, and slim, she would have the same incapacity for intimacy. And, until I accomplished my emotional work, I was doomed to repeat the same pattern of distance. All of us—my girlfriends, wives, lovers, and myself—were incapable of developing the deep intimacy of a healthy, mature relationship. Stunted in our view of adult love, we were adolescent and Disney-esque.

It's normal for teenagers to have visions of knights in shining armor and damsels in finery, like something out of a Victoria's Secret catalogue. That's the fun of being teenagers and that's the way it should be, but hanging on to adolescent beliefs into adulthood is both unrealistic and immature. It only added to my cynicism and anger when my relationships failed.

Of course, I was angry. Who wouldn't be, as their hopes turned to desperation? Who wouldn't be, when yet another soul mate became a roommate? My relationships were all superficial and intimacy only skin-deep.

Finally, looking in the mirror, my life and relationships were clearly reflected.

"How could I expect intimacy when I held my emotions under such tight control?" I asked Jane at our next session. "How could I open up to someone when I didn't even have access to myself?"

"You are becoming very perceptive," Jane said.

"You were right about something else," I said. "I don't think I could have seen this without some emotional distance from my family. Setting boundaries with them was critical."

"You might have been able to understand the patterns intellectually," she said. "But you couldn't heal without doing the work."

"I guess I'm a lot like my Dad."

"You mean you *were* a lot like your Dad," Jane suggested with a smile.

"Do you think I'm free of those patterns?" I asked. "Do you think I'm healthy enough to date without finding someone to take care of?"

"Do you *feel* healthy?" she asked.

"Healthy enough not to get involved with women who have issues," I said. "But I don't feel completely finished with my work yet. I think I still have some things to deal with. Remember how a couple of months ago I said that I knew my parents had never done this type of work?"

"Yes," said Jane. "You were sure of it."

"Now I know why I was so sure," I said. "My dad's relationship with my mom is just like the relationships I've always had with women. Dad takes care of Mom, feels like he saved her. Maybe he's *still* saving his mom, as well."

"That's pretty common," Jane said. "They have a level of intimacy that works for them."

"I guess," I said. "But I want more than that. I want an adult, mature, healthy relationship."

"Maybe you'll find one," she said.

If someone had tried to explain the dynamic to me before I did my work, I would have thought he or she was crazy. How do you show that the reason your relationships haven't worked is because of the dynamic your mother set up with you as a child? It seemed farfetched. Taught that a "true man" has to take responsibility for his own life, I was not inclined to pin my tattered relationships on my parents, but I was learning that my patterns go way back.

Once, I asked Jane for some parenting advice. Was is appropriate, I asked, to occasionally let my four-year-old daughter sleep in my bed.

"It depends," she said. "Are you letting her sleep with you to make her feel better? Or to make *yourself* feel better?"

That stopped me. "Probably a bit of both," I said. "When I'm tired, it's easier to give in to her."

"Does that seem like a good idea to you?"

I realized that our patterns can be very seductive! Maddy slept in her own bed from then on.

I remembered that, at some point in my late childhood or early adolescence, my relationship with my mom soured after she shunned me. The front seat was no longer available and my younger brother became her pet. Although I was angry then, now I'm thankful. That break most likely prevented me from becoming even more stuck. Mom forced me to let go. If she had continued to use me to meet her intimacy needs through my puberty and beyond, it would have made my break much more difficult; her behavior would have been much more damaging and, perhaps, irreversible. On some level, she realized that continuing our "special" relationship into puberty was wrong and that it had outgrown its appropriateness.

"You said that intimacy is not just about sharing feelings," I said to Jane. "Can we explore that a bit more?"

"The more you control your feelings, the less available you are for anyone, including yourself," she said. "You understand that, right?"

"Yes," I said. "But, when I fell in love, I shared my feelings—very intimate feelings. That seemed like intimacy to me."

"But you said that the intimacy never lasted," Jane pointed out. You said that your soul mate became your roommate?"

"That's right," I said. "Then I felt alone."

"Healthy, mature, long-lasting intimacy is the result of trust and commitment," Jane explained. "You can't develop that kind of trust in one night. It just isn't possible. And sex within a safe, trusting relationship is always better and healthier for both people than when those pieces are missing, regardless of whether you believe in marriage or not."

"You also said there's a difference between intimacy and falling in love," I said. "I've thought a lot about that. I always felt as though I needed the other person, almost to the point of desperation sometimes, because I hated being alone."

"And what does that sound like?"

"Codependency?" I asked. "I heard that term but never really understood what it meant."

"Yes," said Jane. "Feeling desperate to be loved leads to a codependent relationship. Codependent means, well, codependent! Both partners have an *unhealthy* attachment to each other. On the other hand, mature intimacy develops over time, not right away. It's different for everyone, but it does have some common elements."

"Like what?"

"Trust, for one thing."

"Which comes from secure, healthy boundaries, right?"

"Yes, but that's not all," Jane said. "Both people must have access to their feelings, as well. They must be *able* to be vulnerable."

"But how can you be vulnerable and…" I stopped. "You can only be vulnerable to someone you *trust*! I get it. And you can only trust someone who has secure boundaries."

"Maybe you've got it," Jane said. "But keep going…"

"To develop a deep level of intimacy, *both* people have to be healthy," I said. "Both people have the capacity to trust and to be trustworthy. My boundaries got screwed up when I was young. Dad's rigidity and discomfort with his feelings taught me to keep my feelings under control, and Mom's boundaries with me were inappropriate, too intimate. So I never learned the difference between healthy and unhealthy. My relationships have all been with women who had trust issues."

I remembered a line in an old Indigo Girls song, "As the bombshells of my daily fears explode, I try to trace them to my youth." I always tried to trace my anxiety to my youth, but

I could never really see their source. They were invisible to me because I was on an *intellectual* quest for the answer to *emotional* problems.

Once I set the boundaries with my family, my lovers and my vices, the patterns materialized, seemingly out of thin air. Now, I understood why I had to do the work alone. No one could possibly understand and see the patterns unless they started their own work. It would be like explaining color to a blind man.

"Do you think my anxiety is genetic?" I asked Jane.

"I don't know," she said. "Is it still a problem?"

"No, it's mostly gone," I said. "But I realized something else. You could look at anxiety or depression as endogenous conditions and, for some people, I'm sure they are. But I see that most of my anxiety came from stuffing my feelings, from all my anger and grief."

"And you might have had a proclivity towards it," Jane added.

"Yes, but the relationship thing," I said. *"That* wasn't genetic. I don't think I had a genetic proclivity towards finding codependent partners."

"Nature versus nurture?" Jane offered.

"It all sort of comes together," I mused. "Part was nature—my tendency towards jumpiness, nervousness—but the other was set up in my family. The two just fed off each other."

"The most powerful model we have for relationships in our lives is our parents," said Jane. "That's what we learn."

"I don't know if I would use the term 'learn,'" I said. "It's more like we 'incorporate' it. I wasn't aware how much I had incorporated my parents' relationship into my unconscious."

"Right," Jane said. "You were too young."

"So, do you blame your parents for your unhappy relationships?"

"I don't *blame* them," I said. "But I believe they are responsible for modeling a relationship that made me unhappy."

"Interesting distinction: blame versus responsibility," Jane said. "I'm not sure I get the difference."

"Blame sounds like a teenager," I said. "I associate blame with anger. And I'm not angry with them anymore, but they *are* responsible. Just like I am."

"Still not getting it…"

"Look, my daughters are still young," I said, "but they experience my relationships with the women in my life."

"You have women in your life?" Jane joked. "I didn't know you began dating again!"

"You know what I mean," I said. "If I have a woman in my life again, then my daughters will witness that relationship. The way I am with them and the way I am with other woman will influence my daughters' relationships as adults."

"I see your point," Jane said. "And I agree that parents are responsible for their children's perception of healthy relationships, but only up to a point."

"Right," I said. "Up to a point—when they grow up, become adults. Which is different for all of us."

"Are you saying that your parents were responsible for your perception of relationships until you decided to do your work?" Jane asked. "Until you were 45 years old, since that's when you decided to grow up? I'm not sure they would agree with that."

"I'm sure they wouldn't because they don't take responsibility for their kids' relationships," I argued. "My dad says that it is *all* nature, not nurture."

"But you see it differently?"

"Yes," I said. "Only when I became aware of the role they played did I become responsible, especially to my kids."

"To your kids?"

"I can see the things in my family that made me who I was—Dad's inability to show his feelings, Mom using me to meet her own emotional needs—both converged to create a vacuum in my life of needing someone to fill it."

"Codependency," she said.

"Right," I nodded. "So, now that I see the pattern that made me pursue unhappy relationships, I have more responsibility, a bigger burden."

"Bigger burden?" she asked.

"My parents didn't know what they were doing," I said. "But I do. The real crime is to continue the pattern, to pass it on to my children."

I can't let that happen.

The Seventh Truth

The happiness you get when you reach the other side is not the happiness you expected.

" And Job pleaded with God, "How much pain must a man endure to see the face of God?
How much grief and anger must a man bear to come face to face with salvation?"
And God replied, "…more."

—The Bible

"I don't quite see the connection between the way I was raised and my anxiety," I told Jane. "Can we talk about that?"

"Sure," Jane said. "One way to look at anxiety and depression is to view them as problems that people have managing their emotions."

"Okay," I said. "But I still don't see the connection."

"How do you think children learn to manage their emotions?" Jane asked. "Children aren't born with the ability to understand what is and isn't appropriate in situations."

"I get it," I nodded. "Whenever Maddy gets angry or sad, the way I react teaches her if an emotion is appropriate or not, right?"

"Well, that's part of it, but there's more," Jane said. "Lots of parents have problems handling their emotions. Your dad, for example, struggled to hold his emotions inside while your mom struggled to let hers out, to find some emotional nourishment."

"Right, but hold on a minute," I said. "If I set poor boundaries with my girls, then they'll struggle with the same problems in their lives."

"That's part of it, yes," said Jane.

"My parents struggled to deal with their own emotions," I said. "Dad was cut off, Mom was too invasive. Wait…Something, something…"

"What is it?" Jane asked. "What do you see?"

Jane's patience amazed me. "It's so clear," I said. "I don't know why I didn't see this before."

"See what?"

"If parents can't manage their *own* emotions, how can they teach their children?" I asked. "My parents couldn't handle their emotions, so I didn't learn it either."

"Not quite."

"What do you mean?"

"Your parents *did* teach you how to manage your emotions," Jane said, "but not *effectively*."

"Effectively?"

"Stuffing your emotions doesn't work," Jane said. "You ended up cut off from them. And using your children to meet your emotional needs damages their ability to trust. Both actions damage children's boundary development."

"I see," I said. "I see the link! I never learned to manage my emotions so I stuffed them but, when I fell in love, I found an outlet, so I purged them."

"In a way, yes," said Jane.

"So my anxiety and depression derived from not learning to manage my emotions?"

"Wrong again," Jane said. "Inappropriate boundaries do not necessarily cause anxiety or depression, though they sure don't help. Emotional health is difficult to define because it differs for all of us—and from generation to generation and culture to culture."

"What does *that* mean?"

"Look at the corporations you work with," Jane suggested. "You said that showing emotion is a sign of weakness that could open up a can of worms for executives. Yet, in some cultures, showing emotion is a sign of strength. In our society *today*, showing emotion is more accepted than it was in your parents' generation. The problem with many men like your father is that they *lost touch* with their emotions. I don't think that's healthy for anyone at any time."

"Or parents who meet their emotional needs through their children…"

"Your Mom went too far, but remember that most parents meet *many* needs through their children," Jane said. "Look at yourself. You seem to find a lot of purpose in being a good dad to your girls."

"You're right," I said. "It's the boundary that creates problems. I don't get my intimacy needs met through them."

"That's healthy, healthier than many families," Jane said. "Now, do you see why you had to do this work yourself, why I couldn't just give you the answers?"

"Yes, the dynamic set up in my family must be very different from others'."

"In some ways, yes," Jane said.

"All happy families resemble one another," I said. "But each unhappy family is unhappy in its own way."

"Tolstoy," Jane nodded. "I know the quote. Every unhappy family is unhappy for different reasons. That is why every person's process is different. All of us have to figure it out on our own, because it isn't something a therapist can teach."

Younger than I am, Susan is an independent woman who runs her own business. As far as I can tell, she is a healthy, mature woman. She was also the first woman I became involved with after my breakdown. After we became intimate, we eventually realized that the physical thing wasn't working because neither of us could or would commit to anything other than a dating relationship. In time, we concluded that our commitment didn't match our physical intimacy, so we backed away from dating and simply became close friends.

"How's your work with Jane coming?" Sue asked me one evening.

"Fine," I told her. "I think I'm about done."

"Done?" she asked. "Don't people in therapy stay in therapy for the rest of their lives?"

"I'm sure some do," I said. "But I think there will be a time when my work is finished. Jane thinks so too."

"Well, how will you know you are done?" she asked me.

"I don't know," I said. "I think when I'm done, I'll know. There's one last thing I have to deal with."

"What's that?"

"Relationships," I said.

"I thought you dealt with your mom and needing to save women," she said. "Didn't you already cover that with Jane?"

"Yes, but there's still more," I said. "I know I'll never end up in a relationship where I'm taking care of my partner—that part is finished. But, remember, when we first met I told you that most of my life I'd been in a relationship?"

"Yes," she nodded. "You said you were either in one or looking for one. What about it?"

"That is the only piece that I haven't dealt with," I said. "I still feel a strong need to be in a relationship. On some inner level, I feel like I have a space that I need to fill."

"Doesn't everyone?" Susan asked. "I mean, I would like to find someone right for me, but I'm starting to doubt it'll ever happen."

"But it's different for me," I said. "You never defined yourself in terms of relationships but I did. That's something I still have to process."

"And then you'll be done?" she asked.

"Unless something else comes up," I smiled.

After Susan left, I crawled into bed with my glass of wine and the morning's *New York Times*. Thinking about our conversation, I decided that unless I let go of the need to have someone in my life, my work would not be complete.

The next day, I woke up with what seemed like the stomach flu as I was nauseous, exhausted, and had no appetite. But my anxiety level was soaring and, suddenly, I feared for my business, my kids and my health. I called my doctor and described my symptoms.

"Is it serious?" I asked. "Do I have something bad?"

"Probably the flu," he said. "Just wait it out."

After a couple more days of upset stomach and exhaustion, I became convinced that I was dying of a terminal disease—then it hit me. I recognized my symptoms and I did not have a terminal disease or a stomach flu. I had the same thing I'd had for the last two years: grief!

I was confused and angry. How could I have done all this work and be back at the beginning again? *How unfair!* I thought. I couldn't even pinpoint the source of my grief, couldn't put my finger on the triggering event. I wanted to call Jane but she was traveling in Europe for a month. I had to deal with it on my own.

I remembered her advice: "Trust your psyche. Trust the process."

Once again, I let go and let the feelings wash over me.

When the grief was exhausted, the truth revealed itself as it always had. That night with Susan, I had made an intellectual decision to let go of my need to have a partner again.

But being in a relationship—finding someone who would make me happy—was my holy grail. Sure, I had given up my quest, but only intellectually.

How quickly I'd forgotten the clues! Letting go is *not* an intellectual process. I had to let go—*emotionally*—of my need for someone in my life, and true letting go is a grieving process.

Exhaustion, loss of appetite, upset stomach were not the symptoms of influenza but simply the result of deep, emotional work. And, then, when I gave up resisting the required emotional work, anxiety rushed in. While the process resembled all the other times of the past two years, understanding this did not make it any easier; the grief was still painful. But, now, I saw it for what it was: *the end of the process.*

All that time I had thought I would end up in a happy, healthy, mature relationship. Now that I was at the end, I realized that my goal was unattainable; only by giving up my most cherished desire would my work be finished. It was the ultimate irony, a cosmic joke.

"I'm sorry you had to go through that alone, Steve," said Jane after her return from Europe. "Were you able to figure out what triggered the grief?"

"Yes," I told her. "I was letting go of ever being in a happy, healthy relationship."

"Why would you want to let go of that?" she asked. "Doesn't sound like something to let go of!"

"Well, maybe it isn't giving up on the possibility of being in a healthy relationship," I said, "but letting go of the need. I want to get comfortable with being alone."

"I agree," Jane said. "*Needing* a relationship isn't healthy but *wanting* one is different. Everyone *wants* someone, unless you're a hermit or a monk."

"The Buddha was right," I said.

"The Buddha?" Jane said, looking confused.

"Yes, the second noble truth of the Buddha is that our desires cause us pain," I explained. "My desires caused *me* pain. I see that clearly now. I kept searching for someone to take care of, someone to complete me. That's what I clung to."

"What do you mean?"

"Everyone has a unique desire," I said. "The Buddha calls it our attachment. For me it was a relationship. Like women who want to be married or have a child before their biological clock goes off. Most of my male friends dream of financial independence or the perfect woman. Others can't make a commitment because they're attached to their independence. Anyway, we all have our attachments."

"Does the Buddha tell you how to free ourselves of our attachments?" Jane asked.

"That's the thing," I said. "The third and fourth Noble Truths teach letting go through meditation. I look back at this therapy as my process for letting go."

"And what do you see?"

"My process was just one long letting go," I said. "Mostly letting go of *control.*"

"Yes, but for you it was letting go of the *illusion* of control," Jane said. "That's not the same thing."

"Funny you should use the word 'illusion'" I said. "That's very Buddhist of you. Buddhists use the term 'samsara' to describe the false way we see the world. The true reality is hidden from us until we transcend our illusions."

"Sounds like a good metaphor for the process we've been through," Jane said.

"When we started two years ago, I just wanted to eliminate my anxiety and depression," I said. "I didn't expect to have to come this far to be healthy. I am a bit skeptical though…"

"About what?"

"About being in a mature relationship, even if I *am* healthy."

"Why?"

"Do you think I'm healthy enough to be in a mature relationship?" I asked.

"Yes, you are," she said. "And you deserve one, after all the work you've done."

"But that's the problem," I said. "I don't know anyone who's emotionally healthy. Every woman I've ever been involved with had problems. I don't know *any* healthy, mature women. Here I am, all grown up, and I don't know any women who are even close to ready for a relationship."

"They're out there, Steve," Jane said.

"How can you be so sure?"

"Can you trust me one last time?" she asked.

"Of course," I said, thinking about "one last time."

"I've seen it happen over and over," she added.

"Seen what happen?"

"You aren't the first to go through this process, you know," Jane said. "You aren't my first patient to cover this ground. I've have patients that did the work you've done and they all got what they wanted in the end."

"All of them?"

"Yes, all of them," Jane said. "But it never matched what they *thought* they wanted when they began the journey."

"What's *that* mean?"

"You came in here wanting to stop your anxiety and depression," she pointed out. "And you did the work to heal yourself, but you got so much more. You got your life back."

"Sure," I said. "But we were talking about meeting someone who's happy and healthy."

"You may, and I hope you will," Jane said. "Remember what I told you when we first started this two years ago? Our first appointment after the hospital?"

"Yes," I nodded. "You said that, if I did the work, I could be happy. That gave me such hope."

"Are you happy?"

"Yes," I said. "Very happy."

"Then I leave you with one last thing, Steve," Jane said. "All your emotions—anger, love, hate, joy, sadness—they are all part of life. To reject them is to reject your humanity. Now *go*," she said. "Enjoy your life."

And we were done.

In the parking lot, as I opened my car door, a wave of sadness washed over me. I felt sad, thinking of the cost to my family and myself for having put off growing up for so long. Feeling an odd mixture of pride and guilt, I looked back over the past two years and understood the distance I'd come.

I started my truck and drove towards home. It was a late fall day and the sun was setting behind the Olympic Mountains. I drove to a bluff where I had a spectacular view of the mountains and the dark waters of Puget Sound. Parked there, I sat and watched the sun slip behind the gray peaks as the clouds' red and yellow streaks faded to light blue and then to dark navy. The windows of my truck began to frost up. It would be a cold night in Seattle.

I glanced at my dashboard clock and wondered whether an hour had really passed while I watched the setting sun. *Time flies*, I thought. Then it struck me that, for that entire hour, I had been unaware of my thoughts. All that time, I did not feel anxiety or worry, and I hadn't fidgeted, but simply absorbed the heavy silence and beauty of the Northwest.

Turning my truck toward home, I realized how much my life had changed in the past two years. I always knew where I was going and what I would be doing; I always had my life planned out. Now, I didn't.

I started to become concerned with my ambiguous future. But, then, I noticed that the clouds had cleared and stars were out.

And I forgot to worry.

Forgiveness

"When we love, we make God."

—Maddy

As I was coming to the end of my therapeutic journey with Jane, I visited my parents on the East Coast. They picked me up at my hotel and we caught up on life over dinner together. Mom told me which friends were coping with what diseases and my Dad told a couple of jokes. It was great. As they dropped me off outside my hotel, Mom gave me a hug. "We love you, you know?" she said.

"I know that, Mom," I told her. "I've always known that."

"Well," she added, "we just wanted to make sure you knew it."

"You know, I love you both, right?" I asked. "I've always loved you."

"Of course, we know, Stephen," she said, slipping Tasty Cakes into my pocket.

Dad rose to give me an awkward hug and I hugged him back with a big smile. Mom patted me on the back and I put my arm around her shoulder lovingly. "Thanks for everything," I said. "I mean that."

"Oh, don't be silly! You're the one who paid for dinner," she argued, though she knew what I meant.

I saw something that night that I'm sure they didn't see: We both had reached the same place with each other—forgiveness.

"I'm done with my parents," I said to Jane. "We got together last week for dinner."

"You sound pretty sure of yourself," Jane said. "How did it go?"

"Great," I said. "For the first time, I thoroughly enjoyed being with them. They are so cute and loving together."

"Oh really?" she asked. "No anxiety or anger?"

"None," I said. "Dad's eating habits are still weird and he still tries to control everything, but they're incredible people. They take such good care of each other."

"Why do you think it feels so different?"

"I can't describe it completely," I said. "There's just no more *stuff* in the air between us."

"Interesting," she said, "that you use the term 'stuff.' Can you explain some more?"

"Yeah," I said. "I feel like an adult around them and it's as if they know it. I'm an adult and they treat me like one. And their old behaviors don't get to me anymore. I even let Mom put Tasty Cakes in my pocket. A year ago, I would have seen that as treating me like a child."

"And now?" Jane pried.

"I saw it as loving, even endearing," I said. "What a great Mom."

"How was your dad?"

"He stayed away from delicate issues," I explained. "He didn't ask me about my love life, my career choices…He knows my boundaries."

"And he respects them?"

"I think so," I said. "We had the first mature conversation I can remember, discussing politics and the challenges of governing. We disagreed with each other on some serious issues but we respected each other's point of view. He's a very smart man."

"Sounds mature," Jane observed. "Maybe you're grown up now."

"They've forgiven me, too," I said.

"What do you mean?"

"I was pretty tough on them this past year," I said. "At times, I was downright nasty."

"Like a teenager," Jane stated.

"*Just* like a teenager," I nodded. "I know it must have worried them, especially after my time in the hospital. I must've seemed so angry."

"You *were*, Steve."

"Yeah, I tried not to take it out on them," I said. "But I know there were times when I could have done better."

"You did fine," Jane smiled.

"You know, in spite of my regrets, I feel that it was something that I had to do," I said. "Just declaring that I forgave them wasn't enough."

"What do you mean?" Jane asked.

"Like the searching I did all those years," I said. "Intellectually, I understood my problems but I was afraid of the hard work, wasn't willing to feel the emotional pain needed to heal."

"How does that square with forgiveness?"

"I may have forgiven my parents intellectually," I explained. "But the forgiveness I feel now is so much deeper."

"*Emotional* forgiveness?" Jane asked. "Rather than *intellectual?*"

"Yeah," I said. "Getting the anger and grief out lets me see my folks as people who are doing the best they can, the best they *could*. The stuff in the air between us is gone. What's left is just people who care about each other."

"Sounds like forgiveness to me," Jane said.

My parents are great people. My mom does hospice work, never misses a birthday, loves my children dearly and makes the best chili in the world. Though my dad can be dogmatic and preachy—and he drinks more than he should—he also is a respected university professor and one of the most book-smart people I know. And he loves his children dearly.

My anger with my parents was the appropriate response of a ten-year-old boy who didn't get the love and attention he needed. My grief was the emotion of letting go of my expectations of childhood and adolescence; that sadness was part of my process of growing up and maturing. Both were natural and necessary.

Dad knows I'm proud of my life. Mom knows I am the best single dad my girls could have. We can never go back to the way it was, but that's the way it should be. You can never go back.

And, now, I have room for love—a kind of love I have never felt before. When they come to visit, Mom does my laundry and Dad gets pedantic from time to time, but I don't mind. Our relationships have changed. My parents know where my boundaries are. They know how far they can push before I speak up.

I love my parents but I will no longer allow them to parent me.
I love my parents but I will never feel their embrace like a child again.
I love my parents but I will never allow them to parent my children.
I love my parents but I will never allow them to talk to me like a child.

That part of my life is over. That isn't their role, and I am no longer their son. Though it makes me feel sad, I also feel self-possessed. I am myself.

The last time I visited my old neighborhood, it was great to see the old sights and to connect with old friends. I even walked from my old house to the grade school I attended, and realized that it was a *long* walk for a ten-year-old kid.

As I drove away from the house in which I grew up, I took one last, long look. I knew that I would never, ever come back. That time of my life is over, just like my therapy and searching are over.

Everything in my life up until now has made me the person I am.

I have an incredible life.

Epilogue

After I did my work, I found this article, which is essentially a template of my recovery process. Anyone can use this to aid his or her therapy.

The Biology of Emotions[4]

Redirecting Self-Therapy (RST) for Anxiety and Depression

E. Van Winkle, Neuroscientist Millhauser Laboratories, New York University School of Medicine

Suppressing anger causes a toxicosis in the brain.

All children are born with healthy anger, which is part of the fight or flight reaction. When parents mistreat or neglect us, even unintentionally, they often cause us to suppress our anger. No parent needs to be perfect, but we must be allowed to have justifiable anger. The suppression of anger is more damaging than the trauma itself. It causes a toxi-cosis that leads to anxiety and depression. Even the lullaby, "Hush little baby don't you cry," serves the parent, not the child. Our parents no doubt had to suppress their anger as children, and this self-therapy is for them as well. As adults we unconsciously form codependent relationships, which are re-enactments of childhood relationships, to set a stage for releasing repressed anger and grief. Many of us have sought partners, bosses, and friends who remind us of our parents and have been unhappy in these relationships.

Repressed anger causes anxiety and depression.

There is a flood of anger in our brains. When you learn this simple biology, the self-help measures will come naturally. When anger is continually suppressed, toxic amounts of neuro-chemicals that store repressed anger accumulate in the brain, clogging up neural pathways where memories of our parents are stored. We may not remember the childhood trauma. Our brains periodically try to release the excess neuro-chemicals during detoxification crises, which are excitatory nervous symptoms. Nerve impulses are often diverted through the wrong neural pathways. As a result, anger may be misdirected toward someone who is innocent or partially innocent, or directed inward as guilt or self-destructive thought. Or the diverting of nerve impulses may cause a variety of other symptoms, from anxiety, to mania, to delusions, even to psychotic behavior. Depression usually follows a detoxification crisis. But these detoxification crises, which cause excitatory nervous symptoms, are healing events—the opening of floodgates to release repressed anger. If we mentally redirect anger toward our parents and other past abusers during the excitatory nervous symptoms, more floodgates can open, and this speeds recovery. Our addiction to people (codependency) and overlying additions to stimulants, chemical or psychological, will only slowly subside because, as in homeopathy, these stimulants trigger the necessary detoxification crises.

Redirect anger during nervous symptoms.

Recognize excitatory nervous symptoms as signals the brain is trying to release the neuro-chemicals that store repressed anger. When symptoms appear, do not suppress them, but redirect the emerging anger toward your parents, not in person, but by pounding on a bed and yelling at them while picturing them or thinking about them. You will find many ways to release and redirect anger. An excitatory nervous symptom might be the pounding in your chest when confronting someone in a current interaction. This is neurotic fear and a signal that repressed anger from childhood trauma is emerging. Never try to re-experience the early trauma in detail. You are not attacking your parents, but only the memories of them stored in your brain. You are getting angry at their sickness. Other symptoms that signal emerging anger are anxiety, panic attacks, tremors, palpitations, compulsive thoughts or behavior, mania, insomnia, nightmares, paranoia, judgment, resentments, revengeful thoughts, loneliness, feelings of rejection, and fear of abandonment. Symptoms might be guilt, shame, low self-esteem, or suicidal thought, which are caused when anger is turned inward.

These are all detoxification crises and opportunities to release and redirect anger. Get to the anger and redirect it as often as possible throughout the day. If it would be too noisy to yell out loud, redirect anger by talking quietly in your mind. Parental voices stay in our heads saying things like, "You should be ashamed of yourself." Tell those voices to "shut up!" Symptoms might be cravings for stimulants, sedatives, sedating foods, sex, psychological stimulation, or meditative techniques to quiet the mind. Other symptoms might be misdirected rage or aggressive behavior toward others.

If anger is intense and out of proportion in a current interaction, most of it is repressed anger from childhood and needs to be redirected to early caretakers. Do not direct intense anger toward others in person. Walk away from abuse. If intense anger is triggered in a current interaction, pound on a bed and direct some anger to that person, but mostly to your parents. After releasing most of the anger privately by pounding on a bed, calmly tell the person in the current interaction you were uncomfortable with their behavior. Explain to others that you may over-react during this recovery process.

Memories of other past abusers who were parent figures for you, for example, male or female authority figures, are laid down in common neural pathways, and you will need to redirect anger to them as well. They might include relatives, bosses, doctors, clergy, and officers of the law, other persons in authority, partners, or friends. False notions of God as a judgmental parent are stored with memories of past abusers, and it helps to get mad at God as well.

Mood swings may worsen, but are temporary.

Releasing anger has a fast antidepressant action. You may feel a temporary "high" followed by increased depression or a drug-like sleep. Remind yourself that the depression will lift, or you may be able to trigger a de-toxification crisis by pounding on a bed. Crying often follows, and feelings of grief may last for many months. Headaches, sweating, fever, and other physical symptoms, which are all de-toxification crises, are common.

De-toxification crises will subside.

In time detoxification crises, that is, the excitatory nervous symptoms, will be less intense and less often. If you let go of addictions before using the therapy, including the addiction to sedating foods, you may have a rather dramatic release from anxiety and depression. If you let go of addictions while using the therapy, your recovery may take longer. After publication of the longer version of this article on the Internet, those who had changed their diets to mostly raw food began to share the characteristics of normal persons in a few months. Normal people feel alive but content, are friendly but enjoy being alone, are patient but cannot be pushed around, feel sad but not depressed, and they have a sustainable peace of mind. They are incapable of violence unless in self-defense. They have a relaxed posture, fall asleep more easily, and have a lighter but restful sleep. They work efficiently and seek pleasure when not at work. Short-term memory and concentration are improved. IQ's can soar.

Childhood memories may return, but without the painful emotions attached. Anger when triggered will still be mixed with anger from the past, and it will be necessary to continue redirecting anger indefinitely. Anger will be mild and related more and more to current interactions. Even when your anger is entirely about the current interaction, feel and express it privately, and then confront calmly if appropriate. If you suppress anger, neural pathways can become clogged up again, and symptoms will re-occur.

Physical health should improve.

Toxicosis in the brain results in periodic over- and under-stimulation of the pituitary gland and other control organs, leading to peripheral disease. When the detoxification process is finished, psychosomatic disorders—better termed neurogenic—disappear. Because you will be attracted to healthier diets, you are less likely to get physically sick. If you do get sick, symptoms will be milder. Neural pathways are clear, and the nervous system can do its daily job of detoxification. Eat as much raw food as possible and avoid stimulants, sedatives, processed or overly cooked foods, refined sugar, grains, and dairy products on a daily basis.

Freedom from emotional disorders and addictions will be permanent.

Eventually the fight or flight reaction is restored, and you will have healthy anger and sadness when appropriate. Addictions will cease. By processing your anger when triggered, you will have a sustainable euphoria, which is not a "high," but is best defined as freedom from anxiety and distress. You will be reborn with the capacity to love and be loved.

E. Van Winkle

I was not an abused child by society's standards, but was left by my mother in my crib to 'cry it out' and listened to my father rage, not at me but at my mother, brother, and sister. I learned to suppress my justifiable anger very early. I was an autistic child and in my twenties was diagnosed as schizophrenic and locked for four years on the violent ward of a mental hospital. I spent much of the time in the mattress room raging against the tight sheets of a straight jacket, or I turned my anger inward in suicidal rage. One of the shock treatments didn't make me unconscious, and I felt pain and panic as the electricity surged through my body. It was like being electrocuted, yet still alive. Over the next thirty years I was confined in more than twenty hospitals, re-diagnosed many times, given every drug known to psychiatry, and had serious addictions. At age 60 I was re-diagnosed with major depressive disorder, then manic-depression, and had symptoms of Alzheimer's and Parkinson's disease. In those years in hospitals only one nurse had a sense of what I needed. She came to my room where I was tied to a bed in restraint, untied me, and gave me a tray of plastic dishes. "Throw these at the wall, dear," she said. Had I known to picture my parents on the wall, I might have begun to heal. I wanted to be locked in those hospitals. I never knew why, but it was an 'acting out' of a fantasy—a re-enactment of having been imprisoned in my crib,—and an opportunity to release my justifiable anger toward my parents. When I understood this and used the self-therapy, I recovered permanently. My full-length story is on: Confessions of a Schizophrenic

Disclaimer

The self-help measures are of a nature of advice given in 12-step programs and are not intended for children under age and in the care of their parents without parental permission. The therapy is safe when the anger is redirected and if there are no serious health conditions. It is best not to make changes in work or relationship during the recovery period unless you are in danger. I cannot assume responsibility for any misunderstanding of the biological concepts. If you use this self-therapy you do so at your own risk. This article does not suggest discontinuing professional therapy or the use of prescribed drugs as ordered by physicians. You can begin the self-therapy while using other therapies and on medication. In time you will not need therapy or medication. Please study the scientific article, which provides a basis for the self-therapy. 9/9/99

References.

1   Anxiety Disorders Association of America, 2002.
2   Joanna K. Macy, Mutual Causality in Buddhism and General Systems Theory.
3   For the Burns Depression Diagnosis Instrument, see Feeling Good, The New Mood Therapy by Aaron T. Beck and David Burns.
4   Elnora Van Winkle, "The Biology of Emotions: Redirecting Self-Therapy (RST) for Anxiety and Depression."

11627259R00065

Printed in Great Britain
by Amazon.co.uk, Ltd.,
Marston Gate.